Stanisław Krajewski

Poland and the Jews:
Reflections of a Polish Polish Jew

Stanisław Krajewski

Poland and the Jews: Reflections of a Polish Polish Jew

Wydawnictwo Austeria
Kraków 2005

To Monika Miriam, my Wife

Contents

Foreword

This book is on Jews and Poland, and the relations between the two both today and in the past. I speak not only as an observer, but above all as a participant in Polish and Polish-Jewish life. I present an account of problems from my personal perspective, that of a Polish Polish Jew. This puzzling phrase means that I am a Polish Jew from Poland, or a Polish Jew who is a Pole. To make it clear to the reader where I come from, my personal development is presented in the introduction.

The introduction as well as the other eight essays are adapted from papers published in the past decade (with the exception of one printed in 1989), mostly after the year 2000. They are not uniform in character but taken together they give, I hope, a picture of contemporary Poland's Jewish dimension, together with the historical background of the issues.

Each chapter is preceded with a short note explaining the circumstances in which the original paper was written. The main themes of the essays are as follows.

Chapter 1 presents the challenge of Auschwitz. This is put at the beginning because the topic seems to be of supreme interest for non-Polish readers. I do not give the history of Auschwitz; I present some problems, their roots, meaning and significance. The same remark – that this is not a history book – applies to all the essays in this book.

Chapter 2 summarizes the whole history of Jews in Poland from the present point of view, dealing with the facts, images and stereotypes that are essential for the contemporary perception of Poland and Polish Jews.

Chapter 3 reviews the main controversial points appearing in the relations between Poles and Jews.

Chapter 4 deals with a problem that is still the subject of great interest in Eastern and East-Central Europe, and is virtually unknown in the West, the story of Jewish communists. They used to be relatively numerous and influential, and, in my opinion, this fact implies a moral challenge for Jews. My approach is, I admit, rather controversial.

Chapter 5 is essentially a reprint of a text from the 1980s, published in the USA under my penname Abel Kainer. It is about the Jewish dimension of the justly famous "Solidarność", or Solidarity, movement. Unlike the other chapters, it is not modified (though some footnotes have been added) so that the flavour of that era can hopefully be perceived by the reader.

Chapter 6 is about the influence of the Shoah, particularly its indirect influence, on Jews in post-World War II Poland, and especially in the free Poland of 1989 and afterwards.

Chapter 7 is about the changes in the Roman Catholic teachings on Jews and Judaism in the last decades. I deal with the Church in general and the Polish Catholic Church in particular.

Chapter 8 is about Christian-Jewish relations and, more specifically, the Christian-Jewish dialogue in contemporary Poland.

The last two chapters concern the area that is of special interest to me, the Christian-Jewish dialogue. I am writing these words in the first week after the passing of John Paul II. The whole world seems to have been affected. In Poland, the dying and the death of the Polish pope has prompted unprecedented national mourning. The country has virtually stopped functioning for the week between his death and the funeral. It has brought to the light of the day the best qualities in the people around. Conflicts have been put on hold, even the football (soccer) fans have stopped fighting among themselves. Among many unprecedented occurrences it is worthwhile to mention the special prayer services that Polish Jews organized in synagogues. Asked to describe my feelings, which are, I guess, identical or similar to those of many Polish Jews, I would emphasize warm gratitude to that remarkable man, and deep solidarity with the Polish Catholics most of whom seem to feel themselves to be "orphans." At the same time I feel neither orphaned nor left without guidance.

While I never called the pope either "Father" or "Holy", I have sincerely expressed my admiration and praise of his achievements. They are generally known. It is, however, less obvious that his last years, and in even greater intensity his last days, have brought about another accomplishment; he introduced into public life the presence of an old, handicapped, suffering, and even dying man so different from the young, fit, happy media heroes. And yet he remained a venerable media hero. This unexpected expansion of the category of who is counted among accepted celebrities, is moving and significant to me. In addition to being a university professor, an author, and an active Polish Jew, I am also the father of a handicapped child. But this does not belong to this book.

Warszawa, April 10, 2005, *Rosh Chodesh Nissan 5765*
Stanisław Krajewski

Acknowledgements

In Chapter 2, on Jews in Polish history, most footnotes are due to Mr. William Brand, the translator of my essay for its first English publication. I have slightly expanded or modified some of them, but this makes me no less grateful to him for his contribution.

I am grateful to all the editors of the original versions of the articles used in this volume. They include editors of the books and journals where the texts originally appeared. I would like to mention in particular the following persons whom I have known for a long time: Michał Bron, Elizabeth Cole, Andras Kovacs, Zbigniew Nosowski, Joshua Zimmerman. I am also glad that due to the work on this book I have identified the editor of Chapter 5, Marian J. Krzyzowski.

All the chapters are revised versions, some significantly modified, reduced or expanded of formerly published papers. The consent of the original publishers to use those texts is gratefully acknowledged. I would like to thank the following specifically for permission to reprint the essays.

- for the Introduction, the editor of *European Judaism* where the article "A Polish Polish Jew" appeared in the issue 97/1, pp. 101-107.

- for Chapter 1, Palgrave Macmillan; the paper "Auschwitz at the Threshold of the New Millennium" appeared in *Remembering for the Future; The Holocaust in an Age of Genocides* (Eds) John K. Roth, Elisabeth Maxwell, Palgrave, Basingstoke, 2001, pp. 322-340.

- for Chapter 2, the editors of *Więź*; the article "'Jewish problem' as a Polish problem", appeared in the special English edition of *Więź*, "*Under One Heaven, Poles and Jews*" 1998, pp. 60 - 81 (notes: pp. 338-343).

- for Chapter 3, the editors of the monthly *Dialogue and Universalism* for which the article "Poland and Jews: inescapable issues" was prepared.

- for Chapter 4, Central European University' Nationalism Studies Program; the article "Jews, Communists, and the Jewish Communists" appeared in *Jewish Studies at the Central European University*, ed. by Andras Kovacs, co-editor Eszter Andor, CEU 2000, pp. 119-133.

- for Chapter 5, Marian J. Krzyzowski (Marek Nowak), Director of Business & Industrial Assistance Division, Ross School of Business, University of Michigan; the article "Solidarity and Martial Law: the Jewish Dimension" appeared (under the name Abel Kainer) in *Studium Papers* (a quarterly published by The North American Study Center for Polish Affairs, Ann Arbor, Michigan), vol. XIII, No 2, April 1989, pp. 54-59.

- for Chapter 6, Rutgers University Press, the publisher of the article "The Impact of the Shoah on the Thinking of Contemporary Polish Jewry", in *Contested Memories: Poles and Jews during the Holocaust and its Aftermath,* edited by Joshua D. Zimmerman, copyright 2003, Rutgers University Press, New Brunswick 2003, pp. 291-303.

- for Chapter 7, Michał Bron Jr.; the article "Catholic Church, the Polish Church, and the Jews" appeared in: Michał Bron Jr. (ed.) Jews and Christians in Dialogue II: Identity – Tolerance – Understanding, *Södertörn Academic Studies 5,* Almquist & Wiksell International, Stockholm 2001, pp. 188-201.

- for Chapter 8, Columbia University Press, 61 West 62nd Street, New York, NY 10023, for the permission to include a revised version of the article "Catholic-Jewish Dialogue in Poland: a Difficult Road to Tolerance", in *Protecting the Human Rights of Religious Minorities in Eastern Europe* edited by Elizabeth Cole and Peter Danchin (pages 490-507). Copyright © 2002 Columbia University Press.

Stanisław Krajewski

Introduction: A Polish Polish Jew

My Place

I am one of those deeply assimilated Poles of Jewish descent who have become deeply involved Jews. My development, paralleled by a number of other similar Poles, represents the reversal of an earlier story well-known from history. Whilst in the nineteenth century, and in the first half of the twentieth, more and more Jews assimilated into the majority culture, aspired to rootedness in it, and gave up their Jewish heritage, in the last two decades or so I and others like me have regained the Jewish identities and Jewish knowledge that our parents did not pass on to us. We do not need to aspire to being Polish, because we have been raised Polish. All the complexities of Polish culture are not only completely familiar to us (as was also the case with many of our parents and even grandparents) but they are ours; what was given to us as children has become our element.

Thus to be a Polish Jew living in Poland today is to differ from most Polish Jews who live elsewhere and are Polish only because of their origins. Many of us are *Polish* Polish Jews; Polish Jews who live in Poland, and who treat Poland as their homeland rather than just a place of origin. Most of us want to remain Polish. We need complete rather than schematic views of Poland. This makes us move beyond the picture of Polish antisemitism. We do not ignore the reality of antisemitism in Poland, we feel it. We know that in the eyes of many Poles, Jews still provide much of the mythical explanation of Poland's misfortunes. In fact, since the mid-1990s, antisemitism has become more vicious and visible in mainstream political life than immediately after the revolution of 1989. On the other hand, however, we do feel the existence of pro-Jewish attitudes, popular interest in "things Jewish", and respect for Judaism. Above all, we feel the bond of common experiences between contemporary Polish Jews and their non-Jewish peers. The similarity of our cultural, political, and intellectual situations has been my predominant experience.[1]

Yet I also feel a bond with all Jews; I know that we are parts of the same faith and fate. This is tremendously important to me. All of these reflections are the result of a rather long search.

1 A review of various Jewish aspects of Polish history can be found below, in Chapter 2. And the participation of people like myself in the democratic opposition and the initial Solidarity can be gained from Chapter 5.

My Background

At first my Jewish identity was non-existent. My parents in post-war Poland thought that Jewishness was a matter of the past and in the new communist world of equality and justice it would be irrelevant. Then they realized that this was an illusion, and that communism meant different kinds of inequality and injustice. Their friends were mostly communists, and many of them, I realized later, were Jewish. As a rule, they were non-Jewish Jews. Very few spoke Polish with traces of Yiddish; only such people were considered 'Jewish' in my parents' circle. Generally, Jewish themes were not discussed at home; they were a virtual taboo. The main exception was the condemnation of antisemitism that was mentioned from time to time as something awful. It usually referred to the attitudes and views that Jews should not be given full rights to participate in Polish life. The fact was that such views existed not only outside but, increasingly, also inside the Communist Party. At the same time the Jewish communists formed a sizable part of the ruling elite. This created a tension that exploded in 1968 as an official antisemitic campaign, which was a major experience in my Jewish development.

There was another exception to the absence of Jewish topics at home; I became aware that my parents wanted to know who was Jewish and who was not. My father, who has a "communist *ichus*[2]" used to ritually remark that the fact of someone's Jewishness did not matter, and in fact my parents always treated people based on merit only. I know this was equally true at the university where he was a professor, yet they clearly felt more comfortable if they knew who was Jewish and who not.

[2] 'Ichus' means noble parentage. My father's grandfather was among the founders of the social democratic movement in the late nineteenth century, and later a leader of communists in interwar Poland, as a Member of Parliament. My paternal grandparents were also communist leaders. All of them perished in 1937 in the Stalinist purges.

It seemed that we were not different from everyone else, and this was apparently the aim of my parents and all others like them. That is why they had nothing to tell me about Jewish traditions or Jewish feelings. I know now, however, that important differences remained, probably indirectly linked to our Jewish origins. This might have been the case, with the stress on intellectual and ethical questions. Also, the fact that we were 'believing communists' who thought that any ethnic or religious specificity was to disappear, which was not common even among Communist Party members, set us apart. In particular, we were not Catholic, which was rather exceptional in Poland. Finally and less obviously, we had almost no family; none in Poland, some in Russia, where my parents had spent the war, and some in Israel. My lack of knowledge was so comprehensive that I did not understand the connection between us and Israel.

In my teens I acquired a purely negative Jewish identity; an identity imposed as I learned that antisemitism could be directed against me. This feeling became especially acute in 1968, when the ruling communists staged an 'anti-Zionist' and anti-intellectual campaign. The Jewish communists, and all Jews and liberals, were accused of being responsible for distortions of communism. This was outrageous, but the Jewish communists who in 1968 came to be the main targets of the system of terror, had been among its main architects, and had participated in the previous dirty campaigns. For years I have pondered the question of the degradation of those communists, who were intelligent, sophisticated, devoted to ethical life; having begun with noble intentions, their zeal led them to participate in oppression and crime. My conclusion is that there exists a Jewish share of responsibility, a reason for us, as Jews, to be ashamed. What is more, the "quasi-religious" involvement in communism was an example of a false religion, of idolatry.[3] Does it follow that there exists a true, non-idolatrous religious involvement?

[3] More details are offered in Chapter 4 "Jews, Communists, and the Jewish Communists", below.

My Search

The 1968 antisemitic campaign made it clear to me that Jewishness did matter. I felt the power of the Jewish condition and sensed the apparently unavoidable character of the Jewish fate. Still, I lacked any serious Jewish knowledge.

Acquiring the knowledge was at first a somewhat detached activity. With my wife Monika, I visited many Jewish cemeteries to take photographs, which later formed her books *Time of Stones* and more recently *A Tribe of Stones*. The drive was hers, although she converted only several years later. In order to understand the tombstones we learned some Hebrew and basic Judaism. We had more and more contacts with foreign Jews – it was a deep pleasure to see how similar we were despite the cultural differences.

Later, in 1979, we were among the founders of an intense underground seminar, the "Jewish Flying University". Again, its Jewish and non-Jewish participants were equally ignorant. For the Jews the first aim was therapeutic. It required an effort to learn to be able to say "I'm Jewish" in a normal tone of voice. We also discovered the world of Jewish traditions where I soon started feeling at home. This meant the beginning of a real Jewish identity, one not imposed from outside but derived from a sense of connection. Not in fear but with pride; not an unfortunate ancestry but a fascinating heritage. The Jewish search resulted not only in a connection to the Jewish history and the Jewish people. It was even more important that I found Judaism as a place where my religious needs could be fulfilled. I had obtained a very strong moral education at home but no specifically religious affiliation. I had looked at everything from Buddhism to Christianity. Nothing was sufficiently compelling. Philosophical analysis led to the understanding that in all areas we make unproven assumptions. From that it could be argued that there is a "God of philosophers", and some Christians said that God was none other but the God of Abraham, Isaac and Jacob. I did not see why. Two experiences helped me understand that there is one God who is the God of Abraham, the God of Isaac, the God of Jacob. One experience was existential, and it cannot be described adequately in a short way. I realized that mutual understanding between humans is possible because God is behind both. The other was a realization that the biblical *Shema Israel* is directed also to me personally, and that I am part of the covenantal relationship, whether I want to be or not. This realization was made possible by a study of the Torah in a small group with my friend Michael, a Christian theologian. I realized Judaism was for me. I understood – recalled? – that my soul was at Mount Sinai when the Covenant was made with God.

My Judaism

Some of us began to recreate rituals. We mostly used American books, and occasional contacts. At the first Passover *seder,* conducted in my home by a friend who was more experienced because of his trips abroad, I asked the four questions; I really was like a child. The following year I conducted the *seder* myself.

Gradually, I became a seriously practising Jew. One move, which by most Jews is taken for granted as the first step, happened when I was in my early forties. Circumcision is generally not practiced in Poland, so a number of us went through it at a relatively advanced age, thanks to the New York-based Ronald S. Lauder Foundation.

I have struggled (and continue to struggle) with some traditional Jewish teachings or practices (for example, discrimination against *mamzerim*[4], or waiting for the Third Temple). But the problems they evoke are among those most important for me. I realized that my parents, striving for equality and justice for all, might have something to do with the age-old Jewish Messianic hopes (and this is, of course, the deepest reason for the anticipation of the Temple).

The near total lack of continuity between the pre-war and post-war generations of Polish Jews living in Poland made the challenge more difficult. However the satisfaction from accomplishments was greater. We learned a lot from books, especially *The Jewish Catalogue: A Do It Yourself Kit*, and later from educational activities under the auspices of the Lauder Foundation. Because we could always choose our pace, and our interpretations, there was no need to rebel.

The synagogue in Poland is Orthodox. I have learned to feel comfortable there. The pleasure of studying the Talmud does not make me Orthodox, and the feeling that I share the passion of the founders of the Reform Judaism does not make me a Reform

[4] The children of illegitimate (incestuous or adulterous) unions; the word *mamzer* has the connotations of the English word 'bastard'.

Jew. In America, I feel especially at home among Jews who belong to the intellectual 'left-wing Conservative Judaism'. At the same time I guess that Michael Wyschogrod is right that if we looked for saintly figures we would most likely find them (if at all) among 'right-wing Orthodox' Jews. I prefer more traditional practice and more liberal theology. I feel the closest link to Franz Rosenzweig, in whom I see a brother, and I think that I have benefited more from Emmanuel Lévinas than from anyone else. The problem of the opposition between Orthodox and Reform is slowly being introduced to Poland, but for a long time nobody wanted to create a formal division. We are too few and the existing divisions are already painful. Even more important, I have come to realize that proper reform, be it slight or deep, can only mean a reform *of* a tradition. You cannot start with a reform of an empty space devoid of religious traditions. We need a traditional Orthodox background. Recently, the ultra-Orthodox Chabad movement has come to Poland. This means a new challenge from the right wing for the official synagogue, and for the Chief Rabbi, Michael Schudrich. In addition, for a few years in Warsaw there has been an association, Beit Warszawa, which functions, in some measure, as a Reform congregation.

I feel that the most serious problem in the confrontation of Judaism with modernity is not so much Torah itself or its various interpretations, but the change in the position of an individual with respect to one's group, or indeed groups, and its leaders. We do not have to conform to group patterns any more; we can choose. The choice should be informed, so learning the traditions is necessary, but individual freedom of choice will be with us till the end of times, and hopefully also after the coming of *Mashiah*.

My Involvement

The more Jewish I am, the more I can appreciate others being Christian. Also, my Christian friends, especially those who supported me in my Jewish search, make me appreciate Christianity at its best. Hence my involvement in Christian-Jewish dialogue in the past years, also in association with the American Jewish Committee (I am its Polish consultant). The point is not to forget or ignore bad things. It is, rather, to develop trust that makes possible a discussion of all kinds of topics. I believe that there may be one exception here: discussing the status of Jesus puts us against each other in a necessarily non-constructive way. The dialogue has helped me to become more deeply Jewish. In fact I feel more respected for being more faithfully Jewish. In 1990, I was one of a few co-founders of the Polish Council of Christians and Jews, where our common Polish experiences create an important bond, and later I was active in the International Council of Christians and Jews. More recently, I have been studying and teaching interfaith dialogue at the Philosophy Department of Warsaw University, where I work (my first scholarly specialization is mathematical logic).

I believe that the long-term task for Christian-Jewish dialogue has barely been addressed. For us Jews, it means to form a Jewish vision of Christianity (and other religions) that is based on our traditions, but presents a real Christianity rather than a caricature, and would see in Christians and the Christian churches our partners. Can we create a partnership based not just on our human brotherhood and ignoring religion but in relation to our Jewishness and their Christian identities? This would mean addressing the Christian claim to have a covenant with the God of Israel, which would go beyond the recognition of their role as a practical form of expression of universal, or Noachide, commandments.[5]

[5] More discussion of Christian-Jewish relations and the interfaith dialogue in Poland are in Chapters 7 and 8.

Since the political changes in 1989, I also have been increasingly involved in the *kehillah*, the religious community, and the main Jewish institutions in Poland. My personal preference also led me to newly-formed Jewish groups, including young people from the next generation after me. We all live in the shadow of the *Shoah*, the young no less than the old.[6] On the one hand it makes our lives, and our Jewish involvement, somehow more significant; on the other, we have to rebel against the overwhelming power of that tragedy, and the way foreign Jews suppose it should influence our lives. We want to lead normal modern lives. We feel that we are a beginning of the new chapter, our own, and not an appendix to the story of the *Shoah*. In addition, I believe that Poland should be remembered primarily as the place of many centuries of the most important Jewish creativity, and not simply as the site of the tragic end.

Shoah has been our background. I myself have taken part in numerous ceremonies, discussions, committees creating monuments and commemorations. Its memory must be perpetuated. Yet it has never been the main source of my Jewishness. I find too often that the commendable commemorations and museums of the Holocaust are just that; they play the role of the core of Jewishness. The museums replace the synagogues and houses of study, Auschwitz replaces Sinai. I find this 'cult of the Holocaust' misleading not only because it does not reach to the living sources, but also because it easily creates morally wrong conclusions. The passionate identification with victims can lead young Jews to the idea that they are themselves survivors. Then the picture is: we Jews are the victims, the innocent good people; the others are the bad guys, the enemy, the guilty. While this makes sense in relation to the *Shoah*, it does not do justice to all later situations.

[6] Between 2002 and 2004, I spent a great deal of time working for the American Jewish Committee which, in partnership with the Polish government, helped create an impressive monument on the site of the former Nazi death camp in Bełżec. For an account of many other issues, see Chapter 1 below, "Auschwitz as a challenge".

Interestingly, my contacts with *Medinat Israel*, the state of Israel, were not of major importance at the initial stages of my Jewish search. I visited my family there as a child, but I was too young to feel a personal connection. My later contacts have been quite intense, and my feelings about Israel are very strong. I was among the founders of the Polish-Israeli Friendship Society. I am pleased that my grandfather is buried on *Har ha-Zetim*[7], in Jerusalem, and I hope for great developments there. In the presence of Israelis I try, though, not to express my hopes that Israel would be a better country than any other. Yet I am not a Zionist. I think that Zionism has won because *Medinat Israel* is a fact. Today's Zionism would mean in practice to make *Medinat Israel* the essence of one's Jewishness. I do not think this is the right way. Contacts with Israel are of vital importance. Yet I think that despite all the differences, Israelis have as much problems with their Jewishness as we do. The State of Israel is a part of a larger entity, the Jewish people.

We witness the formation of a post-Zionist era. Almost all Jews are free to go to Israel and most will not. I imagine that even Russia will (barring a major catastrophe) remain the place of a relatively large Jewish community. Of critical importance is the development of creative Israel-Diaspora relations, with freedom of self-definition for all sides. Young Israelis are learning to recognize that Jews are not temporarily dispersed Israeli citizens, a fact that the early Zionists had to deny in order to succeed. This is one of the reasons I used to be involved in the Jewish Forum movement, trying to develop links between Diaspora Jews and Israelis. As the president of the Jewish Forum in Poland I initiated a Jewish identity telephone hotline. We offered hidden, insecure Jews an opportunity to talk

[7] The Mount of Olives; the Jewish cemetery there is considered the most respectable as, according to – admittedly naïve – tradition, the resurrection of the dead will begin there. I have been trying to interpret many of the traditional naiveties as relevant to modern (wo)man, for example in *54 Commentaries to the Torah for Even the Least Religious Among Us*, Austeria, Kraków 2004 (English edition in preparation).

about their problems relating to their Jewishness. Then we helped create support groups, in the hope that among thousands of people with Jewish ancestors some will begin the uneasy journey into Jewishness.[8]

I have travelled the way of assimilation in the opposite direction. Interestingly, in my case, as well as in the case of some other similar Polish Jews, this *de-assimilation* has *not* meant de-Polonization. We are culturally Polish; we remain Polish Polish Jews.

My initial hopes, however, that Poland's Jewish community could have tens of thousands of active members have proven unfounded. The community grows, but its chances for survival are unclear. There are also growing internal tensions. I feel them, live them, and attempt to console myself that this is the Jewish condition, too. But Judaism is hope. Above all, I hope that Polish Polish Jews will never disappear from the Jewish world or from Poland.

[8] More details about those initiatives are included in Chapter 6 below.

Auschwitz As A Challenge

Abstract

Auschwitz is increasingly important as a symbol: it is a challenge to all of us. How should the site of the former death camp look? How is the camp to be remembered?
One problem is a specifically Polish controversy: Was the fate of all the inmates identical? In Poland, the answer is often that yes, all suffered in a similar way. We must therefore address the question whether Auschwitz is one symbol or many symbols in one.
Some controversies – that of the Carmelite Convent or the field of crosses – have been resolved. Others, such as the church in Birkenau or the Papal Cross, continue to stir debate.
The general problems, disturbing not only from a Jewish perspective, are the following: "de-Judaization" of the site, "banalisation" of the crime, and the anonymity of the victims.
Most disturbing are the attempts to instrumentalise Auschwitz, including a tendency towards Christianisation of the site. It is either the result of ill will or, more often, a consequence of the dominant Christian way of commemorating the victims (for example singling out "the saints").

All these questions demand a consideration of the many levels of the significance of Auschwitz, a task that is impossible to complete without taking into account the theological dimension. Interestingly, the divisions between those who prefer a religious dimension in their monuments and commemorations and those who do not, are independent of the divisions into Jews and Christians.

The text is adapted from "Auschwitz at the Threshold of the New Millennium", in the volume: *Remembering for the Future; The Holocaust in an Age of Genocides* (Ed) John K. Roth, Elisabeth Maxwell Publishing House: Palgrave, Basingstoke, 2001. An earlier version of this paper, entitled "Auschwitz as a Challenge", has appeared in the author's book *Żydzi, judaizm, Polska* (in Polish; Vocatio, Warsaw 1997) and in the Polish monthly *Midrasz* No 0 (1997); English translations were published in "The Best of Midrasz 1997" (abbreviated version) and in *Dialogue and Universalism* 5-6 (1998).

What should the site of the former death camp look like? How is the camp to be remembered? These questions demand a consideration of the profound significance of that place, a task that is impossible to complete without taking into account the theological dimension.

1. Symbol or symbols?

What does Oświęcim-Brzezinka – or rather Auschwitz-Birkenau – mean to us? (I believe that it is better to use the German name in order to distinguish the once normal Polish localities from the terrible places created by the Nazi Germans). Regardless of whether we remember that period or were born decades later, Auschwitz is a trace, a cemetery, a place of remembrance, a museum, and, most of all, a symbol. What does it symbolise? The answer depends on where we pose the question. Everywhere outside Poland the camp is a major symbol of the Holocaust, the Shoah, the mass murder of Jews by Nazi Germany, carried out as part of the campaign to "cleanse" the world of Jews. In Poland, this meaning of the symbol is known by many but not by all, and Auschwitz is seen primarily as a symbol of Polish martyrdom during the German occupation. Precisely because it is a prominent symbol, or even a double symbol, the mode of its preservation, remembrance, and explanation remains such a great challenge.

Let us ask first: Is Auschwitz a suitable symbol of the Holocaust? On the one hand, a number of reasons can be given to say that it is. In the first place, we are dealing with the scale of the phenomenon: over a million people were murdered in what was a true death factory. Secondly, there was the impeccable organisation, large-scale transport (given priority even at the cost of other war and civilian efforts), and the infamous camouflage measures ("showers" in the gas chambers). Thirdly, one remains astonished by the modern scientific methods of organisation of labour and technical innovations (including killing by Zyklon B, which in itself became a symbol of Auschwitz). All these elements are the reason why Auschwitz can hardly be compared to past acts of extermination, even those conducted on a huge scale.

On the other hand, we could question the role played by Auschwitz as the principal symbol of the Holocaust: the camp was also a forced labour camp, and its "products" were not only death but also labour, especially in the Monowice chemical works and other enterprises which together formed Auschwitz III. Together with the original camp, Auschwitz I, and Birkenau (Auschwitz II), they formed an enormous, diverse camp complex. Should it be treated as one entity? In Poland, some people have attempted to recognise Birkenau as a symbol of the Jewish Holocaust, and Auschwitz I as a symbol of the Polish ordeal. True, for the first two years, the inmates of Auschwitz I were chiefly Poles, and later the immediate killing of Jews from transports took place primarily in Birkenau, the site of the main gas chambers and crematoria. Nonetheless, Jews were found everywhere, and during the war these camps constituted a unity, under joint command. The name "Auschwitz" referred to that larger entity.

Furthermore, a relatively large group of people survived Auschwitz. Perhaps a more appropriate symbol of the Jewish Holocaust would be Treblinka, which was exclusively a death camp, whose victims were almost as numerous as those of Auschwitz, and which almost no one survived? Well, I feel there is no sense in posing such questions. Symbols of this kind are not devised intellectually, but appear independently of anyone's specific plans. How? The foremost reason should be seen in the relatively large number of camp survivors; mass extermination of transports ceased during the last few months prior to liberation in January 1945. In those last months there were no more gas chambers. On the day of liberation, there were 7,000 survivors. Some others survived the death march to Germany. Much earlier, when Auschwitz was still used mainly as a prison camp, some inmates were discharged and returned home. It is extremely important that the Auschwitz survivors included among their number such talented writers as Tadeusz Borowski, Primo Levi, Elie Wiesel and others. Is the presence of so much excellent literature among Auschwitz accounts the prime reason for endowing the camp with the rank of a symbol?

Whatever the causes, Auschwitz is and will remain the symbol of the Holocaust and of the "age of crematoria." The very term functions in a symbolic dimension when used in such expressions as "theology after Auschwitz" or in such statements as Adorno's that "It is a barbarity to write poetry after Auschwitz." Everyone has to come to terms with this state of things since this cannot be changed. For the same reason, however, one cannot negate the fact that Auschwitz possesses a second, Polish, symbolic meaning, and that there are grounds for it since the camp played a special role in Nazi policy directed against the Polish nation. Already during the war, the word "Oświęcim" in everyday speech denoted a terrifying place where one could find oneself for actual or alleged crimes against the occupying forces.

Goodwill can only mean the acceptance of *both* symbols. In my opinion, they can co-exist instead of competing with each other. Such co-existence remains mostly ignored abroad where little is known about the Polish meaning of Auschwitz; similarly, in Poland, only recently has an awareness of the Jewish dimension of the place become more widespread.

2. A Polish Controversy: Was the fate of all the inmates identical?

Was the Auschwitz-Birkenau complex a concentration camp whose inmates were degraded until they perished or was it a death camp? This is the sort of question that should remain unasked. Obviously, it was both the one and the other. Unfortunately, many commentaries as well as numerous disputes concerning the "ownership" of the camp are the consequence of posing precisely such questions and the ensuing diverging answers.

In Poland, it is sometimes silently presupposed that the camp was "only" a very cruel prison, most often leading to death of its inmates. The "welcome" speech of the camp commander contained the declaration that "Jews are entitled to live two weeks, priests - a month, and others - three months." These words are quoted to prove that priests were persecuted almost as badly as the Jews. In some sense this is true. Martyrs among clergymen deserve to be remembered and honoured. But this is not to say that the wartime fate of the clergy was comparable to that of the Jews. The very fact of being a priest in a Polish or other town occupied by the Germans was not tantamount to a death sentence, but to be a Jew signified exactly that. Even more importantly, for most of the existence of the camp, its Jewish inmates were those few members of Jewish transports who had passed initial selection. The majority of Jews were victims of immediate murder and not of the horrible concentration camp. The same cannot be said of clergymen, and thus the comparison is misleading.

A similar Polish reaction is produced by the statement that the child victims of the camp were either Jewish or Roma. After all, following the outbreak of the Warsaw 1944 Uprising, over 10,000 residents of the capital, including children, were detained in Oświęcim. Their recollections serve to demonstrate their "ownership" of Auschwitz. Once again: the history of their suffering, which cannot be forgotten, is part of Auschwitz as a prison camp, a place of detention, of starvation and destructive forced labour. There can be no comparison, however, with the fate of Jewish children. Not only was their number incomparably larger but they were, as a rule, murdered in the gas chambers on the day of their arrival. They were not inmates of the concentration camp but victims of the death camp.

The most frequently encountered and most heated controversy concerns those Polish inmates who were not Jews. Many still live in Poland. They recall terrible past events like the deaths of their friends, and the selections that directed the weaker and the sick to the crematoria. The threat of death loomed constantly, and the inmates were endangered and exploited regardless of their origin or religion. "Why distinguish the Jews?" they ask. "We went through the same, we starved, we died. There was no difference between us then, why create one now?"

Polish public opinion has been strongly influenced by the reminiscences of Polish Christian inmates and their conviction about the identical nature of their fate and the lot of Jews. Such a stand is the outcome of tragic and unforgettable experiences. I am by no means inclined to question the truth contained therein. But this is not to say that the thesis about the identical character of the fates of different categories of the victims is true.

There existed some differences even among the inmates: Christians, unlike the Jews, had the right to receive parcels. The most important factor is, however, the difference of background experiences. The Jewish prisoners were those who managed to escape death on the very first day of their detention. As a rule, on that same day they lost many members of their families, sometimes their whole immediate families. This was the beginning of the camp ordeal, incomparable to the fate of the non-Jews. For the "Aryans", Auschwitz was "only" a labour camp, destructive and potentially fatal. Their families usually remained free. The Jews perceived Auschwitz as a death camp, frequently the site of the passing of their entire families. No one waited for them outside the camp, and no one prayed for them. Even if their subsequent camp experiences resembled those of the other inmates, their fate remained different.

For a Jew, the camp number tattooed on his or her forearm signified good fortune, the avoidance of instant annihilation. For a Polish non-Jew, it denoted the worst version of life in occupied Poland. It is difficult for most Poles to understand that "to become a number" could be a reason for satisfaction.

The consequences of those differences of approach became apparent with full force during preparations to the fiftieth anniversary of the liberation of the camp, celebrated in January 1995. Former inmates living in Poland hoped that the ceremonies were to be their festivity. Many expressed (quietly) their discontent that so much was being said about the Jews and not enough about their own history. "We all suffered in the camp!" they argued. For them, Auschwitz was a camp of inhuman life, but life all the same. The greatest misunderstanding occurred on the occasion of the visit of an unusually large group of heads of state. The Polish survivors obviously presumed that the leaders of the world were coming to see them and to pay tribute to their suffering. In contrast to that approach, all over the world Auschwitz remained a symbol, or even the, symbol of the Holocaust. In 2005, during the sixtieth anniversary, with over thirty heads of state, the tension was less acute, though this was probably the last big occasion for the former prisoners to be present together with the leaders of the world. The reason for less trouble seems to be, partly, because the pre-eminence of the Shoah in world consciousness is better understood. Still, only a minority in Poland understands that there were two vastly different categories of victims: the prisoners and the Jews who were immediately gassed.

It is essential not to see the importance of the mass murder of Jews as a sign of ill will towards Poles or of ignoring the suffering of others. The elementary truth is that concentration camps – places of inhuman slave labour and death by starvation – do not constitute an exception but a rather frequent image, encountered in numerous places on Earth, and in different ages. Certain camps of this variety existed quite recently in front of our very own eyes, and who knows whether they are still not in existence. If Auschwitz were "only" such a camp, it would not have become a symbol, and the anniversary of its liberation would not have gathered so many heads of state. It is by no means my intention to offend anyone or underestimate the suffering of any of the camp victims. I am simply trying to demonstrate that the uniqueness of Auschwitz and the source of the symbolic significance of its very name throughout the world is the outcome of its identification with the Shoah. And the fact is that this particular camp was a death factory, a place of a mass-scale, outright, "conveyor belt" murder of entire transports of Jews – children, women and men, the young, the elderly, and mere infants.

3. Controversies: What Should Exist There?

Because of its symbolic power, Auschwitz has been the focal point of many conflicts, some of which have revealed general problems.

3.1. The Carmelite Convent

Among the most infamous conflicts, which sometimes assumed the form of bitter struggle, the foremost was the controversy concerning the Carmelite convent. The whole issue seemed to me to have been avoidable, if enough good will could have been mobilised. Still, one can doubt whether the actual clash of interests, even if only symbolic ones, could have been avoided. The affair was certainly unfortunate since it led to a situation resembling a civil war. Nonetheless, it had at least one positive effect: both in Poland and in the world it stirred interest in the meaning of the disputed site and its future. The storm around the convent disclosed problems more important than the presence of the Carmelite nuns.

Originally, in 1984, I did not oppose the presence of a contempl ative Carmelite convent in the building of the so-called "Theatergebaüde", or "theatre building", just outside the fence of the Auschwitz camp. The Jewish community had not been consulted on the decision but the location of the convent did not meet with objections on the part of Polish Jews, and no one felt that it was part of some wider campaign aiming at belittling the Jewish meaning of the camp. This stand – and the feeling of innocence on the part of the Polish Catholic Church – is best evidenced by the fact that in 1984 an appeal to build a Capuchin chapel in Sobibór, another death camp, was published in *Folks Stimme*, a Jewish periodical issued in Warsaw. Surprisingly for the Church, the reaction of Jews abroad was vehement: the convent was recognised as an offence and a threat. It was accused of being an offence since for centuries the Church had propagated antisemitism and, the argument went, had not offered help during the war; therefore, it should have kept clear of that site. The convent was accused of being a threat because it would falsify the history and the message of the camp, by concealing the Jewish nature of the Holocaust, and contributing to its "Christianisation." Outside Poland, the facts about the victimisation of the Church in the camp were largely unknown. These facts include the Polish symbolism of Auschwitz, the wartime persecutions of Polish clergy (hence the presence of priests among camp victims), and post-war anti-Church repression (it took the Church years of effort to obtain any presence in the area of the camp from the communist authorities).

Initially, I saw three arguments in favour of the initial location of the convent, in the theatre building. Firstly, Auschwitz was not only a Jewish camp; secondly, it became a lively tourist centre and hence there was a need to include some element emphasising another, higher dimension; finally, the building occupied by the convent was located outside the barbed wire fence (I assumed, possibly naively, that the presence of the convent and Catholic symbols would not be expanded to the camp proper so as to include the area inside the fence, a move which I would have found unacceptable). I know many Jews who did not oppose the convent, especially if they were familiar with the topography of the camp. It was my belief that truly important problems, such as "de-Judaization" that is, the hiding of the fact that the large majority of victims were Jewish, could be fought jointly with such allies as the open-minded members of the Church, interested in a Church presence within the camp.

The violent progression of the conflict pushed all those arguments to the realm of abstraction. Both sides revealed much ill will and insensitivity. The critics of the convent wished to protect the sanctity of the largest Jewish cemetery and the memory of the Jewish martyrs rather than to slight the Christian victims or the suffering of Poles. For the Poles, however, such protest had a different meaning. The defenders of the convent were interested in safeguarding the sanctity and rights of the Church and the memory of Polish victims, and not in questioning the importance of the Holocaust, although this was exactly the way their stand was seen by the Jews.

Fortunately, a compromise solution was found, and on February 22, 1987, high-ranking representatives of the Church and Jewish communities signed an agreement in Geneva. They recognised the exceptional nature of the Jewish tragedy (only Jews died only because they were born Jews), and at the same time emphasised the scale of Polish suffering. It was decided that suitable commemoration would entail building, in the course of two years, a Centre for Information, Education, Meetings and Prayer, to which the nuns would be relocated, and which would be situated near the camp. Unfortunately, two years later, on February 22, 1989, nothing had changed in Oświęcim, and protests re-emerged. There was a bitter conviction that the Polish Catholic Church seemed to ignore the signed agreement. This attitude led to the emotional but pacific demonstration carried out by Rabbi Avi Weiss from New York, which Cardinal Józef Glemp described as an "assault" dangerous to the nuns, a declaration that led to a libel suit against the Cardinal. This brought no progress as regards the erection of a new convent building. Despite the fact that initially Polish bishops tried to oppose the project, they ultimately expressed their support, though at first only formal – the original date of building the centre was shifted several times. The construction was completed during the first post-communist government of Tadeusz Mazowiecki, thanks to funds supplied by Western churches. It became apparent that resistance to moving the convent was so strong among representatives of the Polish Church that it had to be overcome by direct Papal intervention. It also became obvious that the Carmelite mother superior was by no means an ally in the struggle for the true image of the camp. In an interview for a Polish American periodical, she expressed openly antisemitic views and a conviction that the Geneva talks were conducted on the part of the Church by Jews. Finally, on June 30, 1993, the day of the relocation of the convent, she handed the building over to a suspect nationalist War Victims Association; the municipal authorities took the case to court claiming that, in accordance with the lease contract, the nuns had no right to introduce new tenants. The case remained in court for years and, in 1999, the Association invited Catholic extremists to reside there (see below: The large cross and additional crosses). At the same time I am pleased that those nuns who decided to move several hundred meters to their new convent are fulfilling their mission of contemplation in an unsullied atmosphere.

On January 17, 2005, after several years of attempts to create something constructive in the building, an educational center, to be connected to the State Museum at Auschwitz, was announced during the events marking the sixtieth anniversary of the camp's liberation, by two former prisoners: Władysław Bartoszewski from Warsaw and Simone Veil from Paris.

I would like to stress that while initially I was not opposed to the location of the convent, I have always shared the concerns and fears that lay at the bottom of Jewish protests (see below: Not Only Jewish Concerns).

3.2. The Church in Brzezinka

Since 1983, the church in Brzezinka has been located in the (renovated and expanded) former SS building, on the other side of the road adjacent to Birkenau, or Auschwitz II. The cross on its roof is visible in a many parts of the camp. The very presence of the church is objectionable to many Jews and has caused protests. Although formally the building remains outside the camp, it is a fragment of the camp complex. For years, its connection to the camp was ignored. This was, I believe, part of the efforts made by the local inhabitants to return to normal life, undisturbed by the wartime heritage. It is easy to understand that they had enough of restrictions resulting from the fact that the Germans decided to build a death factory on their land (which was confiscated from them), but it is difficult to share their opinion.

For outsiders, the very view which stretches in the immediate vicinity of the church, the exotic and, at the same time, disturbingly familiar landscape composed of barbed wire and remnants of dozens of barracks, is so vividly eloquent that the attempts to recreate normal life must cause astonishment. Since this is an exclusively Polish and Catholic form of life (while pre-war Oświęcim had a large Jewish population), for many the return of normal life to areas adjoining the camp confirms the fear that the Jewish dimension of the camp would be disregarded. I know that since the 1990's the Polish directors and staff of the Auschwitz-Birkenau museum have shown much more respect and understanding for this dimension than had been the case in the past. Nonetheless, I am still unconvinced that the local residents and local-government authorities really understand the nature of the problem. Also, while almost nobody seems to be deeply distressed by the presence of the church, I am puzzled by the fact that the local Catholics do not feel that they should find another location for the parish church, not in the immediate vicinity of the barbed wire.

3.3. Crosses in the "Field of Ashes" in Birkenau

The case of the other crosses in the camp became generally known after a speech given by Elie Wiesel on July 7, 1996, during the commemoration of the fiftieth anniversary of the Kielce pogrom. The moment chosen by the speaker was highly unfortunate since the stormy debate around the crosses overshadowed the Polish attempt to face the pogrom and the resulting moral challenge. Wiesel protested against the presence of "religious symbols" on the ashes of Birkenau, and described the existing crosses as "offensive" although he did not deny that they could have been placed there as a result of good will. The majority of the audience did not realise that he called not only for the removal of the crosses but also of similarly sized wooden stars of David. These symbols had been installed ten (!) years earlier when the area was tidied by a group of young people from Warsaw. The directors of the museum *de facto* agreed to the presence of a dozen or so temporary crosses and stars, a strange decision considering that normally they refused any sort of private symbols of remembrance. For some time, the symbols in the "field of ashes" included crosses with a "crucified" Star of David. Regardless of the original intention, such unconventional symbols produce disturbing associations: the Jews as a redeeming sacrifice, and the cross as the instrument of the tragedy of modern Jewry. The combined symbols were removed rather rapidly.

The field of ashes mentioned by Wiesel is situated in a part of Birkenau that is distant from the main gate, and rarely frequented by regular visitors. It contains the ashes of victims, mainly Hungarian Jews, murdered in 1944 and burnt on pyres, owing to the insufficient capacity of the crematoria. These technical details have a cold ring to them, but Wiesel found this site to be extremely laden emotionally, as it was the resting ground of his closest relatives. Even if a part of the ashes are not remains of Jewish victims, most of them are, and they are scattered everywhere. This is why crosses are inappropriate. They falsify the true character of the site, the argument goes, and would not be chosen by the deceased just as they are rejected by their families. The fact that the ashes are not only Jewish means that neither Jewish nor any other religious symbols are suitable, argued Wiesel, whose view is probably shared by a strong majority of Jews.

In December 1997, all the symbols, eight crosses and eleven stars of David were removed from the field of ashes. This was possible due to co-operation of the government, the local bishop, leaders of the International Council of the Auschwitz Museum, and leaders of seven major foreign Jewish organisations that formed a task force. The action was conducted in a respectful way: the crosses were put in a church, the stars in the Jewish Historical Institute. The solution met with both approval and opposition. Clearly, few moves at Auschwitz can meet with universal acceptance.

It must be admitted that that compromise step – the removal of both Jewish and Christian symbols – was made easier by the fact that Jews do not regard the stars as indispensable. The site itself is a sign and a symbol. It is enough if we remember, as we must remember.

3.4. The "Gravestone" of Edith Stein

At Birkenau there is another site that I find upsetting, though it is little known to the wider public. Some inscriptions have been placed on extant fragments of the so-called "Biały Domek", or "little white house", situated in the field of ashes, which also served as a place of mass murder. These inscriptions, commemorating Edith Stein, are another private contribution to the iconography of the camp, permitted as another exception (once again I am unaware of the reason); they constitute the only remembrance of a specific individual in Birkenau. This situation is difficult to accept not only because of the outstanding but controversial person commemorated, but also because the exception was made. I believe that one may honour either each specific person proposed by concerned visitors or no one in particular. Otherwise, arbitrary decisions are imposed, which unavoidably introduces an accidental and, at the very least, one-sided vision of history.

3.5. The So-called "Supermarket"

The case of the so-called Auschwitz supermarket became widely known in the spring of 1996. After articles in local Polish press, there were protests all over the world against the project of a shopping complex to be built by a German-Polish company near the camp entrance. The venture did constitute an attempt to profit from the presence of great numbers of visitors. The company purchased a suitable lot and, in addition, opened its offices in the building of the former convent, which it leased from the nuns. The whole affair sounded highly disturbing. There was, however, little real reason for protesting.

I have no doubts that it would be best for the area in the direct vicinity of the camp to remain empty, and for outside activity not to disturb the solemnity of the spot. Nonetheless, the Oświęcim museum did not protest, and it had good reasons for acting in this way. In the first place, the terrain, also the one adjoining the controversial investment and building, was by no means empty and it still contains numerous shops, wholesale warehouses, and firms, located both in pre-war buildings and in tacky barracks built long after the war. Secondly, the new construction would adapt and expand the existing building, without causing a visual deterioration of the site. Thirdly, refreshment stands and a fast food bar have been situated next to the camp entrance and even within the camp for many years. The new building was supposed to take over their functions and thus make it possible to remove the bar and the shops; also, the existing parking lot would be relocated; ultimately, the project would improve the overall situation.

The whole issue is, in my view, the result of a misunderstanding. People unfamiliar with the area surrounding the camp envisaged the appearance of a great construction site, disturbing the atmosphere of the site. The ensuing affair was unworthy of such an emotional outburst. It did, however, recall the true problem: contrary to the intentions of the local authorities, the area encircling the camp cannot be made part of ordinary life. It seems to me that the local authorities did not quite appreciate the great attention with which the camp area is watched by the whole world, and not only the Jewish community. The seriousness of the situation was understood by the Polish government, which stopped the construction works and declared that the entire terrain around the camp would be put into order under the direct surveillance of Warsaw authorities. In fact, consultations with the above-mentioned coalition of Jewish organisations (including, among others, the United States Holocaust Memorial Museum, Yad Vashem, the American Jewish Committee, the World Jewish Congress, and the Ronald S. Lauder Foundation), gave rise to legislation putting all former death camps under special government protection. This time, a controversy with oblique beginnings produced something constructive.

Unfortunately, the tension between Warsaw representing 'the world', and the local residents has not been overcome. The co-owner of the former supermarket, Mr. Janusz Marszałek, was elected the mayor of the town in 2002.

3.6. The Large Cross and Additional Crosses at the Gravel Pit

The controversy concerning the Carmelite convent brought about another one: a large seven-metre-high cross (22 ft) in the garden of the convent, that is the "theatre building", about 40 yards outside the barbed wire fence. The cross was placed there on July 26, 1989, during the peak of the controversy over the convent. Under that cross (but in another place) John Paul II had celebrated a mass in Oświęcim in 1979. It was then stored for ten years and erected at night by a group of local Catholics, led by a local priest, Father Stanislaw Górny, with no authorisation from Church leaders. The cross, situated in the former gravel pit where executions of 150 Poles had taken place during World War II, was justified as a memorial to those victims. Normally, however, symbols of that size are not installed. It is obvious to me that it was put there as another act in the "religious war," to spite "the Jews".

The controversial cross remained in the garden of the convent, and when, in 1993, the nuns were relocated it seemed obvious that the Church authorities foresaw its relocation in the wake of the convent. I heard about such plans from competent bishops. However, no move followed. The prolonged fight over the legal status of "the theatre building" and its garden hampered further steps. No less important, among Polish politicians and Church leaders there was a fear that any move would infuriate the "defenders of the cross". These maintained that in Poland crosses can be put anywhere in order to express the religious feelings of the overwhelming majority of Poles. Critics of the location of the cross have maintained that its presence alters the character of the place, contravening the conditions of the 1979 inscription of the Auschwitz site on the UNESCO register of world heritage.

Personally, I always regarded the cross as more disturbing than the convent. The presence of the convent could have remained discreet and for all practical reasons unnoticed by visitors – this was the case originally and, I hoped, would remain so – but the presence of a giant cross is overbearing. It towers over that particular fragment of the camp, annexing its space and upsetting the visitors. Obviously, that was the prime purpose of situating it there.

In Spring 1998, it seemed possible that the big cross would be relocated. Public protests were issued that the relocation would constitute a profanation of the symbol of the cross. In March, a group of 130 parliamentarians signed a statement defending the "Papal cross". In June came a new phase of the affair. Catholic extremists, led by Kazimierz Świtoń, started planting new crosses, up to four metres tall, around the big one. Soon there were dozens of them and several months later over 300 crosses of all sizes were present.

The place became a rallying point for extreme Polish nationalists, often displaying madly antisemitic views. In the leaflets they distributed they accused the Polish government and bishops of being Jewish or at least Jewish lackeys. Some of their leaders were under influence of the schismatic Church established by Archbishop Lefebvre. Thus the activists could hardly be seen as representing Poles in general. The bishops stated that the action by the "defenders of the cross" was unjustified. Still, the extremists did express widespread feelings: the need to commemorate Polish suffering, the connection to the Polish meaning of Auschwitz, and respect for the symbol of the cross. Only a minority of Poles supported the idea of a radical police action against the extremists who illegally occupied the garden of "the theatre building." The government several times pledged to move. In March 1999, a new law was introduced (in 1997 it had been announced in a declaration, signed by the Polish authorities and an international Jewish coalition, headed by Miles Lerman), which established a hundred-metre protective zone around the camp, under the direct control of the government. Świtoń, who had been living in a tent at the gravel pit, was arrested under this law on May 28, 1999, and all the new crosses removed. The action was prompted by the imminent visit of John Paul II.

The large cross remains where it was put in 1989. Similarly to the convent affair, a considerable amount of quiet international diplomacy was done. The most promising compromise seems to be a screening solution: while the cross would remain, it would not be seen from the camp proper if a screen were put between it and the barbed-wire fence, e.g., a wall or, preferably, a cluster of trees.

4. Not Only Jewish Concerns

Notwithstanding critical opinions about some of the Jewish protests and the forms they assumed, I always shared the basic anxieties that led to the protests. I mean primarily "de-Judaization", or a "banalisation" of the crime, the anonymity of the victims, and a tendency towards Christianisation. All these attitudes were, and to a considerable extent continue to be real, profound challenges.

4.1. "De-Judaization"

It is relatively easy to overcome the official "de-Judaization" of Auschwitz. For decades, the fact that the overwhelming majority of camp victims were Jews, who perished only because of their origin, was ignored. The Oświęcim museum, guidebooks, and school textbooks mentioned victims from twenty-eight nations, whose alphabetical list began with Austrians and ended with Jews (in Polish "Żydzi"). Such descriptions totally disregarded the fact that most and sometimes all the victims from various countries were Jewish. This shocking falsehood was supported by the entire system of communist propaganda, and pointing it out was tantamount to launching an attack against the authorities. Thus, it is not surprising, though still unjustified, that no protests were voiced abroad throughout the whole period of the propagation of that lie. Decisive progress took place after 1989: the new museum exhibitions mention Jews from the very outset, and the guides talk about the Jewish victims; changes were introduced into commentaries to the documentary films shown to visitors. Also various protests, possible in the now free Poland, made a contribution to the new atmosphere, which has space for the true story of Jews at Auschwitz.

From the very beginning, this issue became the domain of a special commission established by the Ministry of Culture in 1989; in 1990 it was transformed into an International Council of the Auschwitz-Birkenau Museum. The commission quickly closed some of the so-called national pavilions, arranged by governments of different countries many yeas ago; they included the Bulgarian and East German pavilions which displayed chiefly the history of the local communist parties. At present, the Museum staff enjoys contacts with the West and Israel, and, being well familiar with their goodwill, I firmly believe that all omissions can be made good, yet a more basic problem remains.

Responsibility for the concealment of the Jewish dimension of Auschwitz lies upon the communist authorities, as well as associations of former camp inmates, in the past dominated by communists. The Church, frequently accused during the more recent controversies, is not to blame, because it had little influence. Still, the fact remains that the communist lie was widely accepted. Did it not make it easier to accentuate the Polish meaning of Auschwitz considering that, apart from Jews, the largest group of victims were Poles, that is, Polish Christians?

In a press interview, the Carmelite mother superior emphasised the fact that the camp victims came from twenty-eight countries and that, therefore, the Jews exaggerated their bond with the site. Reports made by Polish Christian former camp inmates also express the attitude that the Jewish dimension is not special. In the 1960's, during a school excursion, I learnt that Oświęcim was the site of Polish martyrdom and not a single word was spoken about Jews. The typically Polish rivalry (with the Jews) as regards suffering was being won by forgetting about the Jews. Generally speaking, the memory about Jews in Poland was, and still often remains inconvenient. In addition, as Henryk Grynberg has noted, the victims are posthumously Polonised most eagerly by the persons who would have opposed the right to Polishness of those victims when they had been alive.

4.2. The Number of Victims

The verification of the total number of victims could be reliably accomplished only after 1989. The earlier binding number of four million was determined initially by a Soviet commission after the liberation of the camp, based on estimates of the burning capacity of the crematoria. No one dared or wished to question it. For years, this was the figure cited uncritically in textbooks, guidebooks, and articles published throughout the world. It was also inscribed on the central monument in Birkenau where plaques in nineteen languages informed visitors about "Four million victims of Nazi murderers."

For quite some time now it has been obvious to specialists that four million was a greatly inflated number. Not until the 1970s was research started in the West and Israel for the purpose of determining the true number. Final calculations cited a figure of one to one and a half million, of which about ninety percent were Jews. This was by no means an easily acceptable figure. Apparently, many persons think that a lower number of victims can diminish the importance of Auschwitz and the suffering of its inmates. But it is exactly the exaggeration that deprives all efforts at commemorating the tragedy of their reliability. It also assists theses propagated in the West (marginally) and the Arab countries (officially) by the so-called revisionists who negate the existence of the gas chambers and the genocide of Jews. Moreover, several million victims would signify that, apart from about one and a half million Jews, millions of non-Jewish inmates, mainly Poles and Soviet prisoners of war, lost their lives. If that were the truth, then Poles would constitute the majority of all victims. This is possibly the reason why some people have grown so attached to the larger, false number.

The established figures of those murdered in Auschwitz-Birkeanu are: between 900,000 and 1,000,000 Jews, 75-80,000 Polish Christians, over 20,000 Roma and Sinti (or Gypsies), 15,000 Soviet POWs, and others.

4.3. The Anonymity of the Victims

The monument commemorating the victims of fascism was unveiled at Birkenau in 1967. I have always regarded it as a much greater problem and offence than the convent that drew the attention of so many people. Erected on the site of the Birkenau crematoria, the memorial made no mention of the Jews and did not contain a single Jewish motif! Recalling the victims (four million), it kept them totally anonymous. The omission of the word "Jew" could have been avoided if not for ill will, but, at the same time, there came to the fore a much deeper problem, more difficult to overcome. It is easy to speak about millions of victims, but it is difficult to imagine them. Overcoming the anonymity of victims in our memory appears to be a moral commandment. It is one of the most important challenges posed by Auschwitz. Victims constitute a nameless mass, but we should remember them as individuals with unique faces. Reading about the history of the camp, one can easily envisage several persons hung for their crimes but how are we to imagine hundreds of thousands being gassed? Paradoxically, the camp commander Hoess is remembered much better than his victims.

To me, the text on the main plaque of the memorial at Birkenau is the most offensive element of the monument. Almost no one in the world has paid attention to it, probably because it is written only in Polish. The text says that the "Council of State of the People's Republic of Poland" awarded the "Order of the Grunwald Cross, First Class, to the heroes of Oświęcim who died there, struggling against Nazi genocide for the sake of human freedom and dignity, and for the peace and brotherhood of nations." Once again, the victims remain anonymous, and the only name mentioned belongs to a state institution which no longer exists. This is highly distasteful. The order awarded to "the heroes" is glaringly unsuitable for the tragedy of the gas chambers. It would make sense if it referred to members of the camp resistance movement and not to all victims. The words about the "struggle for freedom and dignity" would then also possess concrete meaning. Against the backdrop of the whole phenomenon of Auschwitz, they sound awkward: the inmates did indeed fight for dignity, some even for the dignity of others, but much more often they just struggled to survive. More important, victims of the gas chambers did not struggle for anything, even for survival, and had no chances for waging such a battle. The monument's inscription ignores them completely, and thus relegates their tragedy to oblivion. After all, it was they, those innumerable crowds of Jews, who should be recalled on the ruins of the crematoria. Of course, I believe that members of the camp resistance movement as well as participants of escapes and acts of rebellion should be honoured and commemorated, and that the victims of those events deserve special remembrance. Nonetheless, the overwhelming majority were innocent, helpless people and not fighters. It is they who must be honoured by the main monument. And the misleading text is still there!

4.4. The Banality of Evil

How should the camp be presented? I remember that after visiting the camp with my school class I experienced a feeling of horror but, at the same time, of unreality. Auschwitz resembled a museum. Is it only scale and proximity in time which distinguishes it from a display of torture instruments featured in a mediaeval castle? If we disagree with this opinion, then we face the task of telling this to young people. How to avoid the threat of rendering the site and its message banal? The place can become banal through our behaviour, conversations, tourist services and even exhibitions. The presented image could create the impression that killing millions of persons is easy, that it only requires suitable organisation and technology. We are left with an impression of the frailty of moral arguments, a feeling of helplessness and anger. Can we do better?

I know that in the case of groups of Israeli youth their rage and hatred towards the perpetrators do not always find a vent. If their guides are insufficiently sensitive to these emotions, then the visit to Auschwitz can result in an animosity towards the world, Europe, and the Church, which could become easily transferred from abstract concepts to more concrete and closer representatives – the Poles.

I feel sometimes that evil is still radiated there. The camp's functioning was based on dehumanisation. When we describe those times now we often unwillingly adopt the perspective of the perpetrators; for example, when we use the term "extermination", we automatically compare the victims to vermin, which the Nazis did consciously. That is why I avoid the dehumanising term, and prefer to say "mass-murder."

5. Threat of "Christianisation"

The suffering of Poles during the German occupation was so hard that for the survivors and their families this dominates their memories. For two years Auschwitz was a camp for "political" prisoners, mainly Poles. If this group included Jews it was not because they were Jewish. This was to come later. The Polish symbolism of Auschwitz, which I mentioned above, is the result of actual tragic experiences. Ignorance of this fact abroad produces a bitter reaction in Poland. Poles find it difficult to examine problems posed and symbolised by Auschwitz upon the level of Christian-Jewish relations. For Poles – and to some extent also for Polish Jews – Auschwitz belongs to the realm of Polish-German relations.

Basically, when thinking about World War II, Polish Christians perceive suffering shared with the Jews rather than a Church shared with the Germans. While this community of suffering is often mentioned with good intentions in order to show appreciation for the suffering of Jews, in the Jewish experience such a community never existed. During the first period of the occupation a community of this kind was a fact, but the persecutions of Jews soon reached an incomparable level. Without underestimating the tragedy that affected all Poles, it seems worth recalling that the possibilities of survival were not comparable.

A Jewish child had virtually no chance to survive, while a non-Jewish child, despite real threats, enjoyed a considerable chance for survival, even in Warsaw. Despite this, in Poland the Holocaust is interpreted as a fragment of the sufferings of the Polish nation. In this way, the Shoah's challenge to Christianity remains mostly unrecognised. This fact results not only from experience but also from a Polish Messianic tradition, which claims that the Polish nation suffers as the "Christ of the nations." Hence, the suffering of others cannot be greater or more worthy of reflection. Since the Jewish source of such thinking is also alive, one should not be surprised at the persistence of the "rivalry in suffering." This historical context makes it difficult for us to perceive Auschwitz as a challenge for Christianity.

What is this challenge? To put it bluntly, it could be described as the need to see the camp as a place where Christians murdered Jews. Such an interpretation appears to be a misunderstanding. After all, the murderers were Christians only by name. Clergymen were found among the inmates, and not among the guards. Many Christians and even antisemites perished. I believe that such a direct accusation of Christianity is mistaken and, even if it is justified by despair and anger, it remains abusive.

Still, one could enquire about the role that the antisemitism of Christians – and more, Christian antisemitism – played in shaping the mentality of the camp guards and in preparing the ground for the Holocaust. One could also ask, as many Jews do, why the camp functionaries were never threatened with excommunication by the Churches to which they nominally belonged? Such questions provide us with the justified interpretation of the challenge that Auschwitz constitutes for Christianity. They should be also reflected in the camp museum.

Certain Jewish worries could conflict with the Christian approach. Whenever I speak about specifically Jewish concerns, I do not maintain that they cannot be experienced also by Christians. There are such Christians, as well as there are Jews who understand Christian approaches. I understand the need for the presence of the Church at Auschwitz. I also believe that while seeking ways for expressing the truth about Auschwitz Jews can, and do have allies among Christians. The concealment of the Jewish dimension of Auschwitz must be blamed not on the Church but on the communist authorities. Nonetheless, I still believe that "Christianisation" is a genuine threat.

The prospect of the "Christianisation" of the appearance of Auschwitz and its memory is becoming real not because of the ill will of the Church. Some Jews think so but actually the problem is different. Even if there is no ill will, the difficulty remains, because the Christian way of commemorating the tragedy causes Jewish opposition.

It is a traditional Christian reaction to place a cross or crosses, or holy figures, on the site of a tragedy. The intention of this act could be to honour Christian victims but also to honour the ashes of other victims. I myself respect this attitude, being well aware of the fact that those intentions can be totally pure. If, however, the same act is performed in a place that conceals the ashes of innumerable Jews, we cannot accept this. Anyone can pray. Christian prayers pose no problem (Jewish visitors have witnessed such prayers on numerous occasions). With sufficient good will, Christian ceremonies could express understanding for Jewish sensitivity and pay homage to the Jewishness of the victims. On the other hand, I consider placing crosses and other religious symbols as an annexation of the area. Such behaviour reveals the expansiveness of Christianity. Although at present the Church drive for expansion remains restricted, the legacy of history is clear: for centuries the presence of crosses indicated the power of the Church. It also signified discrimination against Jews.

We, Jews, do not find the erection of stars of David or other symbols particularly important. In his Kielce speech in 1996, Elie Wiesel expressed this sentiment by opposing all religious symbols in the Birkenau field of ashes. The site itself is a sufficiently eloquent symbol. The absence of all signs is regarded by the Jews as much better than the joint presence of Christian and Jewish symbols. In addition, if we were to be consistent, then a red star should be added for the communists, together with a number of other symbols. Should this be the correct path for commemoration, then it would require careful and extensive consultations with all interested parties in order to decide on the nature and number of the signs and their location. It would be also necessary to take into consideration the proportions of the numbers of respective groups of victims, and to reach an agreement regarding the pattern of commemoration: whether one could apply the model of a military cemetery, where graves and symbols co-exist, or the model of a predominantly Jewish cemetery (as is the opinion of most Jews), or, finally, whether solutions proper for cemeteries should be employed in the case of Auschwitz at all. The issue is difficult, and it would be easiest to choose a compromise and not to place any sort of signs apart from religiously neutral information.

The arbitrary placement of crosses based on the conviction that the cross is a universal symbol expressing the emotions and hopes of every victim is erroneous, and reflects Christian triumphalism. I can understand the Christian wish to make the cross the symbol of the supreme values for all people. This is, however, wishful thinking, and not reality. Jews perceive the cross as an ominous symbol, traditionally a threatening one. Comprehension of this fact is reflected in a noteworthy fragment of the July 1996 declaration by the Committee for Dialogue with Judaism in the Council of the Polish Episcopate, and signed by Bishop Stanisław Gądecki. Obviously, today many Jews experience no strong emotions when they encounter a cross; also, most Jews are perfectly aware of its lofty meaning for Christians. Still, the memory of persecutions remains, as well as a feeling that the cross represents an alien and unacceptable religion.

As long as a certain symbol is not universally accepted as a symbol of reconciliation, it must not be imposed upon others.

The problem of "Christianisation" is more profound than the threat of the domination of Christian symbols. It is also present in the possibility of the domination of Christian, or actually Catholic, saints.

The Church has tried to deal with the above-mentioned question of the anonymity of victims. It did so in a characteristic manner, by canonising two camp victims: Father Maksymilian Kolbe and Sister Teresa Benedicta of the Cross, that is, Edith Stein. In no way do I question the right of the Church to take such steps. Obviously, I do not share the Catholic cult of saints, but I recognise the fact that this has been the only successful attempt to overcome that anonymity. I have nothing against the worship of those two persons by the Catholic Church. Both are outstanding people, and Kolbe's heroic death and the impressive personality of Edith Stein deserve our deepest respect. Nevertheless, the outcome of this Church initiative is highly disturbing: representatives of the camp victims have been created. And they are by no means typical victims! Catholic saints cannot be representative of victims whose overwhelming majority were Jews. A Catholic priest and a Baptised Jewish woman lend their faces to people whose identity was completely different. This situation would have been bad even if Kolbe's name had not been associated with antisemitic publications, and if Stein's name had not evoked a rejection of Judaism. Edith Stein was an exceptional woman who became a nun and died as a Jew. I know that some people of good will assume that she can symbolise all the victims. This is not the view held by most Jews, for whom she recalls conversions to Catholicism, a painful issue, especially in the context of Auschwitz.

Is there a solution? It is impossible to create Jewish counterparts of persons whose likeness would be sold in kiosks and elevated onto altars. There is no such tradition in Judaism. An informal remembrance of particular Jewish victims is possible but that would make no essential change in the situation dominated by the images of those two particular saints. I can only fervently hope that all those who co-create the cult of St. Maksymilian will constantly recall, both to themselves and to others, the existence of other kinds of victims.

There exists a threat of "Christianisation" even subtler than the domination of Christian saints. I have in mind a specific Christian approach to the sense of suffering, and thus the resulting perception of the sense of the camp. Sense or nonsense? From the Christian point of view, one immediately thinks of the redeeming quality of suffering. In the Jewish tradition, such a link is not at all obvious. The most pro-Jewish Christians easily compare the Shoah to the suffering of Jesus and hence they treat the Holocaust, in accordance with the literal meaning of this term, as a sacrifice performed on an altar. This approach suggests some noble aspect of sacrifice. Then, we ask: who carried out that sacrifice? No answer can be satisfactory, and almost every response is offensive. The Christian interpretation endows death in the gas chambers with more meaning than is acceptable to the majority of Jews.

Similar objections appear even in the case of indirect suggestions. Some French Jews accused Andrzej Wajda of ending his film "Korczak" with an unreal, poetic scene of the children escaping the transport, which amounts to a suggestion of their victory over death. The critics saw this scene as disrespectful to the children murdered in Treblinka, and even as an expression of concealed antisemitism. In my opinion, their charges were unjustified; they used the film as a pretext rather than an object of critique. Nonetheless, numerous Jews regard such "Christian" optimism as illegitimate. Also, the optimism of a "Zionist" interpretation (children thrive in the State of Israel despite Treblinka) is questioned by some Jews. Even John Paul II, whose sensitivity to the Jewish fate is indisputable, declared that such great a suffering as the Holocaust must bear equally great fruit. This belief is acceptable in itself but, in my estimation, finds the redeeming sense of the Shoah much too easily. Auschwitz contains no redeeming element that is usually connected with the concept of martyrdom for the faith. It constitutes an ultimate horror because Jews were condemned regardless of their readiness to defend the faith, and regardless of their behaviour.

There are many forms of instrumentalisation of the Holocaust. "Christianization" is one example. Other examples are provided by those Jews who introduce other versions of the concept of sacrifice. Thus, according to various opinions, Jews died to absolve the sin of Zionism, or of insufficient Zionism, or of other "unsuitable" ideologies. I have the impression that for most Jews no imposition of any indirect meaning of martyrdom is acceptable because it brings almost a justification of the perpetrators and it slights the victims.

6. Involuntary Theology

During the first years after liberation, the camp functioned as a hospital and then as a prison for political prisoners, Germans and Silesians. In 1947, a museum was created, administered by former inmates. Everything was familiar to them, and evoked nightmares rather than metaphysical fears. The crimes were obvious. Preservation of the evidence and the conservation of details were not considered a priority. Most of the wooden barracks were pulled down for fuel by the army and the local inhabitants. The authors of the museum were concerned with depicting the place, the suffering, and the experiences of the inmates. No theological analysis was attempted, even in the West. In the East, the communists, who had constituted a large part of the camp resistance movement, turned Auschwitz into a symbol of fascist crimes; it was also used to document the merits of the "progressive" Socialist countries.

The present-day museum staff and commentators of the tragedy as well as the average visitors know about Auschwitz only from reports. Soon there will be no more eyewitnesses. In the West, a growing number of people deny the very existence of the gas chambers. The first attempts at Holocaust denial also occurred in Poland in 1999. Therefore, the image presented to visitors, or pilgrims, must be adequate and convincing. It must have sense both now, in fifty years and, I suppose, five hundred years from now.

There are two basic visions of the appearance of the camp in the future: one, information-educational exhibitions, with the use of computer techniques, or two, leaving the entire site as it was, with no alterations. I am certain that in practice both proposals must be taken into consideration. Since information is indispensable why not use modern methods? On the other hand, the further from the camp one lives the more need to maintain the site "as it was" is emphasised. Such a requirement is, however, a myth, and although its implementation would be highly desirable, it is impossible. Despite the awe that it produces, Birkenau simply does not look the same as it did in the past. It has trees and grass, which could not grow during the camp's existence, being stifled by thousands of feet; the whole camp has assumed an almost bucolic appearance. Many of the objects would have collapsed had they not been conserved. New barbed wire replaced the old and even the crematoria ruins were reinforced with injections of cement so that they would retain their forms. Many objects urgently require thorough conservation; the famous collection of hair cut from the inmates and not sent to the factory that used it as raw material, calls for sophisticated conservation techniques. Central heating, recently installed in some of the barracks, is contrary to the authenticity of the objects but indispensable for their preservation. A large part of the funds for these additional undertakings comes from Germany (once again). The needs exceed the means. Most important, the way in which the museum is to function still remains unresolved.

Is it suitable to pray in the camp? All Christians and most Jews have no doubts that it is. Nevertheless, it seems worthwhile to understand the opposite feelings. A not uncommon Jewish argument suggests that the camp area should remain empty and silent. This silence is to replace all prayers and would be a reflection of the absence of Divine intervention. God allowed horror to reach the very bottom – and turned the camp into a banal factory of conveyor-belt produced death. Speaking about the inappropriateness of religious ceremonies and about responding with silence to God's silence might appear to be the sophistry of Jewish atheists who have no need for religion anyway. However, the issue is not that simple. A more complete theological argument was presented by René Samuel Sirat, former chief rabbi of France, a very traditional man who participates in inter-religious dialogue. His point of departure is a quotation from the book of the prophet Jeremiah: "And they have built the high places of Topheth, which is in the valley of the son of Hinnom, to burn their sons and their daughters in the fire; which I commanded them not, neither came it into my heart. Therefore, behold, the days come, sayeth the Lord, and it shall no more be called Topheth, nor the valley of the son of Hinnom, but the valley of slaughter" (Jeremiah 7, 31-32). This valley of slaughter is now Auschwitz, even more so than Topheth or Ben-Hinnom, where children were sacrificed to Moloch. Thus, concludes Sirat, prayer in Auschwitz is tantamount to participation in a "most terrible idolatry."

Regardless of the value of this appeal for "absolute silence, without prayers and conversations," it remains a fact that almost all Jews, even those who are distant from religious practice, come to Auschwitz to pray. They do want to recite the *kaddish*, the mourner's prayer. Originally, I thought that the resistance against all prayers expressed by those Jews who otherwise are not opposed to religion, was primarily a rationalisation of spontaneous animosity towards Catholic ceremonies. Some of them, however, react with equally spontaneous unwillingness to traditional Jewish prayers. A Jewish survivor of Auschwitz once told me: "I saw how my closest relatives were killed but when I am there I am not able to say kaddish".

Silence cannot be maintained in the whole camp simply because it is visited by crowds of tourists. In my opinion, all the tourist services - gastronomic, commercial and sanitary - should be moved outside the camp. Quite possibly, there is a need to introduce certain rules concerning behaviour, and perhaps even clothing worn in the camp, although the imposition of regulations of any sort is extremely difficult. I do not complain about the visitors. On the contrary, I believe that the enormous interest in this site is not an annoyance but a challenge. More and more foreigners will visit the camp site. Whether one likes it or not, it has become one of the chief Polish tourist attractions, and probably the most universally known place in Poland. The inhabitants of Oświęcim profit from this tourist influx although they complain about disturbances in normal life. Oświęcim also has the opportunity to become a great centre for reflection in a Europe undergoing transformation and unification. The ceremonies of the fiftieth anniversary of the liberation of the camp, though poorly organised, were successful: it was an impressive gathering of heads of state, including royalty. The sixtieth-anniversary ceremony was even more impressive.

The place intrigues because it places before us the most profound dimension of human existence. It is not an easy task to capture it and it is even more difficult to describe it but one thing is certain: all religions refer to this dimension. The religious aspect needs to be introduced in order to express it, and to avoid "banalisation". I believe that this need was the reason for the efforts pursued by the Catholic Church to win the right to be present within the camp. Regardless of the forms of realising such projects, I regard their motivation as justified and worthy of respect and support. My sympathy is not eliminated by objections raised by the fear of "Christianisation." As a matter of fact, most Jews appear to accept prayers in Auschwitz. What is rejected is "institutionalised" prayer, like for example the convent. This is the view achieved at Jewish-Catholic talks about the convent, held in Geneva in 1986 and 1987. Yet, the problem of distinct places of religious cult still remains topical: one of the death cells in block 10 contains a Father Kolbe shrine. The Jewish pavilion has a place for contemplation. Some of the Jewish visitors expressed the need for the display of an object that would constitute a Jewish focal point. From the perspective of Jewish tradition, the most natural would be a plaque with the text of the prayer for the dead. Both the above-mentioned places of prayer are enclosed within buildings. This is probably the reason why they have not met with open protest. Perhaps a number of particular objects could be featured inside camp buildings. There are plans for a display of private plaques and remembrance objects in the former Central Camp Bathhouse (known as the *Sauna*) in Birkenau.

I maintain that the best way to introduce the religious dimension in a universally recognised manner is to resort to quotations from the Hebrew Bible. This conception was the theme of lengthy debates in the International Council of the Auschwitz-Birkenau Museum and Memorial, an advisory body established by the Prime Minister of Poland (initially by the Minister of Culture). The Council decided to replace the unsatisfactory texts on the Birkenau monument with more suitable ones. I proposed a quotation already used on other Holocaust monuments – a verse from the Book of Job (16:18): "O earth, cover not thou my blood, and let my cry have no place." The merits of this text seemed obvious. In the first place, it is forceful and appropriate. Then, the Hebrew Bible is equally important for Jews and Christians. A Biblical quotation automatically introduces a higher dimension in a way understandable to all. At the same time, it is sufficiently down-to-earth not to offend anyone. Furthermore, the Book of Job contains as its central motif the problem that is most important for the atheist viewpoint – the presence around us of the suffering of the innocent! The original is in Hebrew, so when put at the central place of the memorial it would immediately insert the Jewish dimension in a most natural and uncontroversial way. Finally, let us note some theological subtleties: in the original, "blood" appears in the plural, which ancient rabbinical commentaries explain as a reference to the blood of the innocent or else to the future generations, unborn as a consequence of murder. Both interpretations are exceptionally suitable for Auschwitz.

The majority of the Council members, both Jews and Christians, supported the choice of this quotation. We were astounded, therefore, at the protest voiced by the largest association of former camp inmates. Its chairman, Maurice Goldstein from Brussels, a Council member and long-time president of the International Auschwitz Committee, opposed the proposal energetically, calling for a plaque with a more faithful description of the history of the camp and the essence of the crimes. Everyone recognised the need for a true historical description but, first, it would have to be sufficiently long and there was no place for that; secondly, it would make it difficult to include that deeper, or higher, dimension whose absence was felt by all. In the course of informal discussions, Goldstein expressed his ultimate, innermost argument: "There was no God then, so we want nothing from the Bible now". This was an anti-theology, which is itself some kind of a theology.

The negotiations were lengthy; after all, representatives of former inmates must have had an important voice. The final compromise assumed the form of small plaques in twenty languages, with a brief historical description, and the quotation from the Book of Job in the original, Polish, Romany, English, Russian, and French to be put on a large plaque. An editorial committee was established. It became apparent that it would be extremely difficult to write a text that would satisfy all. This is yet another reason why Biblical texts are so valuable: no one tries to edit them.

Ultimately, the small plaques contain the text: "Forever let this place be a cry of despair and a warning to humanity, where the Nazis murdered about one a half million men, women and children, mainly Jews, from various countries of Europe. Auschwitz-Birkenau 1940-1945." This simple inscription appeared six years after the removal of the old tablets with the (false) information about four million victims. In 2005, the main plaque about the granting of a medal for "those struggling for freedom and dignity" still remained unaltered.

We are unable to comprehend fully the solemnity of Auschwitz and of the Holocaust without a dose of theology. The controversy concerning the plaques revealed that it was difficult to avoid such questions as: "Where was God?" or: "Is our image of the tragedy influenced by the fact that Jews are the chosen witnesses of God, an article of faith of Judaic tradition, present in the teaching of the Church?"

One of the most interesting attempts to face the deeper significance revealed by Auschwitz, and to emphasize its religious sense in a non-standard way, is the annual event organized by an international Peacemaker Community, based in New York. Each year since 1996, a group of individuals of various faiths and nationalities spends several days there, meditating, being present at prayers, sharing emotions and insights with others. This approach sharply contrasts with the usual way: a quick visit followed by an immediate departure.

The visitors tend to identify themselves with the camp victims. This is the case not only with Jews, Poles, Americans or Hindus but also, to a certain degree, with Germans. The Austrian pavilion commemorates Austrians only as the victims of Hitler, although so many Austrians supported him and numerous camp functionaries were Austrian. Mention is also made of Slovak victims although the Slovak authorities, on their own initiative, organised transports of local Jews to Auschwitz. How are these complex problems to be presented without propagandising but also without taboos? How is one to avoid simplified answers to the question concerning the identities of those guilty?

Obviously, major guilt is borne by Hitler, his co-workers, organisers of the camp, and its guards. It is an illusion, however, to claim that such a single-stratum answer is sufficient. In a certain sense, the victims of Nazism included also certain Germans assigned to this "job". Also, some prisoners had their contribution to the functioning of the camp. This is why the most penetrating question appears on a purely human level, beyond the divisions into Jews and Christians, Poles and Germans, etc. Basically, we all are the same human beings as the heroes and the villains of Auschwitz. Therefore, we all face the same questions. What behaviour is possible in an anti-world, in which anti-values rule supreme? What to do in order to survive? How important is survival? Consecutive generations of young people must be asked: what would I have done if I had found myself there, at that time? What if I had been an inmate? And what if I had been a guard?

Do we have the moral right to pose such questions? But, conversely, do we have the right not to ask?

"The Jewish Problem" As A Polish Problem

Note

This essay is a survey of the issues in Polish history in which there exist clearly diverging views among average Jews and average Poles. The very first version of the essay, meant for the Polish intelligentsia, was published, under my penname Abel Kainer, in an underground periodical "*Spotkania*" 29/30 (1985), pp. 32-64. A version close to the present one was published in Catholic monthly "*Więź*" in 1992, and the English version in 1998 in a special issue of "*Więź*" entitled *Under One Heaven. Poles and Jews.*, pp. 60-81, together with an addendum, omitted here. Many footnotes explaining Polish history are by William Brand, who added them for *Więź*.

Jews continue to be important in Poland as an issue, an issue that is significant for everyone, and an obsession for some (in fact, for surprisingly many). Jews are now important only as an issue, although many Poles imagine that the Jews are numerous and influential. In the meantime, the Jews hardly exist in Poland as a group. There are, of course, individuals here and there, although the Jews who are important and visible in various fields are usually the people to whom the term "Poles of Jewish origin" is most appropriate. It is hard to say what a given person feels, yet it is easy to ascertain that almost none of the better-known individuals belong to any Jewish institutions, religious or secular, and that they do not meet other Jews in any specifically Jewish forum.

Jews are hardly numerous in Poland, but the attitudes toward Jews are far from indifferent, almost as it was before the war, when the Jews constituted a minority of over three million. One no longer encounters "the Jewish problem" on the street, but this does not mean that it has been consigned to history. Obviously, the "problem" is not as pronounced and in any case, certainly not only associated with the presence of Jews, but also with the attitude to Jews. In this sense, it has been and continues to be a Polish problem.

Antipathies and resentments dominate relations between Poles and Jews. This is mutual. They lead to harmful stereotypes on both sides. It is difficult, however, to treat them as fully symmetrical. One can cite prejudices or point out false judgments on either side – a point here, a point there – but the actual consequences differ. It was Jews who suffered because of Polish attitudes, and not the other way around. Furthermore, although each deserves censure, antisemitism and antipolonism are different by nature. The roots of European antisemitism are incomparably deeper and stronger. They include the beginnings of the Church, the place of Jews in Christian Europe and afterwards in the Europe of nation-states, and also embrace the psychological need for a personification of evil. The psychological needs are similar among Jews. Antipolonism, however, does not result from an overall vision, but rather from a generalization of the Jewish experience in twentieth-century Poland and from the complexity of Jewish history in the Polish lands, where fate – or God – once assembled such a numerous Jewish people.

It is difficult to avoid a certain simplification that appears at once in the very terminology, including that employed by me. Namely, speaking of "Poles and Jews" suggests two separate groups standing beside each other, or even in opposition to each other. This is partially true, but in reality there existed – and still exist – many spheres of interpenetration: Polonized Jews who are active in Polish life and among the Polish émigré community, as well as Poles who live and work with Jews. At times, a division between "Christians and Jews" would be far more accurate: we would then have Christian Poles and Jewish Poles or, as people once preferred to say, Poles of the Jewish faith. I belong to this last category.

1. Poland: Paradise or Hell for Jews?

Asked if the Jews had it good in Poland, the average Jew gives an answer precisely opposite to the answer given by the average Pole. Foreign Jews usually see a dark image full of raging antisemitism, discrimination, and dangers to the peace and even life. Poles, on the other hand, generally suppose that the Jews lived well in Poland, exercised great influence, were wealthy, and so on. This opinion sometimes becomes a conviction that the Jews had it too good in Poland.

Heaven or hell? It is necessary to distinguish between past centuries and our own. The definition "Jewish paradise" applies to the period of the First Republic.[1] Applying it literally or even worse figuratively, to later times is an abuse. Nevertheless, the universally

[1] The "First Republic" was the centuries-old, multi ethnic state that declined in power, efficiency and purpose for more than one hundred years before vanishing from the map of Europe in 1795, when Austria, Prussia, and Russia performed the last of the three last partitions of its territory and King Stanisław August Poniatowski abdicated. Until the mass slaughter of Jews and Poles during the Cossack uprising initiated by Chmielnicki in 1648, in what is now Ukraine, the Polish state had seen a steady growth in Jewish settlement under conditions that, all things considered, were actually advantageous to a degree not found elsewhere in Christian Europe, particularly after the mass expulsions and persecutions of Jews in other countries in the fourteenth and fifteenth centuries.

dark stereotype common among Jews is just as inaccurate as the image of an idyllic Jewish life, not to speak of a vision of Jewish domination. The richness and creativity of Jewish life in this Polish land deserves to be appreciated by those Jews for whom the experience of the twentieth century overshadows more distant history. This is what Rabbi Abraham Joshua Heschel was thinking of when, in New York after World War II, he spoke of a golden age in the history of the Jews.

Jews gradually arrived within the borders of the First Republic, until the great majority of the Jews of Europe were gathered here. The Jews had, after all, been expelled from various countries in the West, while in Poland the worst that happened was their expulsion from some cities. Benefiting from Polish tolerance, the Jews were able to develop more of an autonomous life than elsewhere, although they could not, obviously, go beyond the forms accepted in that epoch. The inferior status of the Jews was due in part to the same principles that covered all non-nobles. They were at additional risk as non-Christians, guilty in general opinion of the death of Jesus and subsequent intransigence, as well as such misdeeds as the profanation of the host and ritual murder. The stable position of the Jews depended mainly on the attitudes of the great and lesser feudal lords. Jews were necessary: they functioned as intermediaries between the nobility and the market, and between the nobility and the peasants. This led to the Jewish-noble symbiosis so characteristic of old Poland.

The opportunities for the ennoblement of converts to Christianity are sometimes adduced to show how good the Jews had it in old Poland. From the Jewish point of view, this is no cause for celebration. Inducements to conversion, whether they are physical or economic coercion or such emoluments as ennoblement, appear as threats. The goal, after all, is to remain Jewish despite the natural course of things, despite history, the dominant nations, and religion. The most general definition of antisemitism as Jews understand it is this: to prevent Jews from living as Jews. Conversions to Catholicism were not, in fact common, and occurred on a wide scale only in the case of the seventeenth-century Frankist sect. The king himself stood as godfather to Jakub Frank, the founder of the sect.

Several generations later, Frankist descent began to be stigmatized here and there as a source of "foreignness." Before the epoch of emancipation in the nineteenth century, however, religion was the only criterion of Jewishness. Baptisms, signifying to both sides a definitive break with Judaism, brought full acceptance. Although the situation later grew complicated, the religious criterion was officially applied until the end of the Second Republic,[2] especially by the Church. Nevertheless, the criterion of descent became more widespread. A dramatic expression of the difference of approaches was the public slapping of Father Tadeusz Puder, Jewish by descent, in his Warsaw church in 1936. For present-day antisemites, the religious criterion has lost all significance: during the 1990 presidential campaign, Tadeusz Mazowiecki[3] and his Catholic intellectual associates were attacked by some supporters of Lech Wałęsa as untrustworthy Jews on account of their actual or supposed Jewish forebears.

All the time, Poland was a center of rabbinical orthodoxy and mystical Hasidism, as well as the Yiddish press, literature and theatre, the revival of Hebrew, modern political parties—socialist and nationalist, with Zionist parties and sports clubs. Such groups en-

[2] The "Second Republic", a Polish nation-state with Jewish and Ukrainian minorities each comprising about ten percent of the population, was formed after 1918 on the territories had previously annexed by the Austro-Hungarian, German and Russian empires. This state lasted until September, 1939, when it was invaded and partitioned along a pre-arranged line between Nazi Germany and the Soviet Union.

[3] In 1989, Tadeusz Mazowiecki led the first non-communist government since the occupation of Poland by the Soviet Army in 1944, when communist rule under Soviet direction was established.

joyed representation in the parliament of the Second Republic. They all developed unhampered thanks to the wide range of freedom that sharply differentiated Poland from its neighbors during the 1930s. Jews also participated, of course, in various non-denominational spheres of national life. They were Polonized to a greater or lesser degree, and those who held important positions in the state or the military were as a rule converts, sometimes in the previous generation – in other words, they or their forebears had in principle broken with Jewish circles. The lack of baptism made even a university career difficult. To an increasing number of Poles, Jewish participation in national life meant that Jews "had it too good." This was expressed in slogans about Jews "controlling" various fields, about certain professions being "in Jewish hands," about culture being "Jew-infested," and so on.

Despite anti-Jewish attitudes, then, there was room for coexistence and even symbiosis, for the Jews of Poland were an inseparable part of Poland. So it had been from time immemorial. Critics of the Jews defined them as parasites. Today, young Poles frequently idealize the pre-war situation and think that there was no antisemitism then. In this view, there was only economic competition, and competition in the professions and culture, because the very numbers of Jews – greater, after all, than anywhere else in the world – caused tension and rivalry. They also stress that anti-Jewish ideas, imported from Tsarist Russia and later from Germany, ran counter to the true nature of Poles. All these circumstances had great significance indeed, yet blaming antisemitism on them is clearly a defensive manoeuvre which irritates Jews and puts them off. On the other hand, they can be taken as a sign that it is currently fashionable to distance oneself from antisemitism – verbally, at least.

2. Antisemitic Generalizations

Antisemitism is obviously not a specifically Polish phenomenon, nor did it originate in that country. A certain attitude towards Jews, it always expressed itself in the form of accusations. These accusations are contradictory. The Jews are thus accused of excessively isolating themselves and of being excessively intrusive, of being offensively different and of making themselves similar to others, of radical traditionalism and unbridled rebelliousness, of economic expansion and of passively vegetating. Furthermore, the Jews of Poland were accused of a lack of patriotism and indifference to the struggle for independence while on the other hand they were also accused even of provoking the January Rising.[4]

Antisemitism is the common denominator of these accusations in the form of generalized opinions. This is not to say that they have nothing to do with reality. There were plainly cases in which they were formulated in good faith. It is, after all, true that some Jews were very traditional, that some were pious while others flaunted religion, and so on. The main thing was that they were antagonistic towards each other. Only in fantasies about an all-embracing Jewish conspiracy did a Jewish banker and a Jewish anarchist report to the same boss. The harmonious integration of contradictory accusations against Jews in general is possible only within a vision in which Jews act in unison against others, and in which their varied involvements are only a mask that enables them to act on different

[4] The unsuccessful January, 1863 Uprising, concentrated in the Polish lands governed by Russia, broke out after several years of unrest. During the preparatory period and the actual fighting, there was significant Polish-Jewish cooperation in propaganda, mass demonstrations and rallies, logistics, finance and clandestine operations. The Jews also suffered disproportionately harsh reprisals after the defeat, including numerous cases of exile to Siberia. Like the other major insurrections of 1794 and 1830, which also failed to win Polish independence despite the shedding of much blood and great sacrifices, the January Rising was afterwards the occasion for profound soul-searching, recriminations, and bitter disputes on the sense of history and the independence struggle.

fronts, but always to the same end: domination over the "goy." This is the antisemitic vision. In reality, Jews were engaged on both sides of most conflicts. This is still the case. In Poland, some Jews supported the government, and some supported Solidarity,[5] in the days of contention between the two forces. Jewish solidarity is a cornerstone of Jewish tradition, but the reality consists of divisions and quarrels. A sense of a shared fate may exist, but, at best, true solidarity emerges only in the face of a common danger. At best – since, for example, cooperation between Bundists and Zionists ran into massive difficulties even during World War II, in the Warsaw Ghetto, in the face of the most extreme danger.

The deeper basis of antisemitism is most clearly brought out in the most radical of the charges against the Jews: the accusation of ritual murder. It is almost shameful to mention such slander, but to this day there are people who remain convinced that there is a secret Jewish ritual for which Christian blood must be found to make matzo. Recent ethnographic research in the Polish countryside found a majority inclined to believe this. In the past, the result could be mortally dangerous. So it was even after the war: the crowd that murdered the Jews in Kielce in 1946 had been incited to the attack by rumours that a boy had been kidnapped to make matzo. The belief in ritual murder had different, tragic consequences during the war for the family of a certain Jewish child who was being sheltered by valiant Catholics. After the war, they refused to return the child to his Jewish relatives – in fear that they would kill him to make matzo.

[5] The "Solidarity" trade union movement arose after strikes in 1980 and grew into a political force boasting millions of members around the country. Its first chairman was Lech Wałęsa. The original "Solidarity" structure was repressed after the communist authorities declared Martial Law on December 13, 1981, and the union was officially disbanded in 1982. Afterwards, "Solidarity" referred to clandestine union structures, and also to the wide social movement which continued in opposition to the communist regime until the fall of the latter in 1989. After the fall of communism Solidarity has functioned as a regular trade union, increasingly right-wing. To me, as to many others, it has nothing to do with the initial Solidarity we participated in.

Other accusations against the Jews may from time to time have something in common with reality. However, the facts are often not so much the source of prejudice, but rather a convenient illustration of it. Jews were once accused of greed, exploitation and dishonest dealing. This charge echoed the old aristocratic contempt for trade and merchants, which only today is being undermined by the sudden acceptance of the businessman as a positive model. Another type of accusation against the Jews had to do with immorality and the propagation of nihilism, promiscuity and all sorts of decadent vices. Instances confirming these charges may be found, but the point is that pre-war publications – of a type again being disseminated in Poland today – presented lifestyles at variance with traditional precepts as the result of a deliberate program to undermine the morals of Christians. This is absurd. The Rabbis were no less opposed to promiscuity, secularization and novel lifestyles than were the priests who criticized Jews on these very grounds. Jews leaving the traditional community were involved in shaping all modern tendencies in economics, culture and science. A spotlight was cast on Jewish criminals out of the belief that Jews are evil and, furthermore, that evil exists because of the Jews. In today's Poland, we have had a taste of such generalizations: Polish tourists have suffered from the generalized opprobrium stemming from the acts of Polish thieves and hooligans in Germany or Denmark.

Today, Jews are seldom accused of dishonesty or immorality. Such charges no longer sound convincing, since everyone can see that dishonesty and immorality have not disappeared, even though there are no longer many Jews in Poland. The accusation of disloyalty is a different story: even today, Polish politicians of Jewish ancestry are accused by their opponents of acting "against the interests of the nation."

3. Jews and Poland

Jews are accused of lack of patriotism and of assimilating to the culture of the powers that partitioned Poland. It is obvious that, while some Jews became Polonized, many chose cultural Germanization or Russification. Many others remained firmly within Jewish culture and had no plans to assimilate. From a Jewish, rather than a Polish, perspective, this is hardly an accusation. Rather, it is the normal course of things. Even the Polish point of view, however, must include circumstances that call into question any unequivocal accusation about a lack of patriotism. In the first place, the accusation is frequently formulated as if all non-Jews were patriotically engaged in the struggle for Poland. In reality, neither the aristocrats nor the magnates (not to speak of the kings!) were any less cosmopolitan than the Jews. Among the peasantry, a national consciousness independent of loyalty to the local landowner and the reigning monarch took root only gradually, and generally not before the nineteenth century. (As late as twenty years ago, one could find old highlanders who, speaking in the dialect of the mountains, identified themselves as "Austrians.") It is indeed a fact that Kościuszko[6] found adherents among the peasants, but it is true as well that he also found supporters among the Jews, whom he addressed in the Krakow synagogue. Actually, it must be said that a relatively large number of Jews took part in the Polish fight for independence. This was principally the case at the time of the January Rising and somewhat earlier. A part of the religious leadership was also involved, as symbolized by the head rabbi of Warsaw at the time, Ber Meisels. In general, however, many centuries of experience had left the Jews,

[6] Tadeusz Kościuszko, a hero of the American War of Independence, initiated an Uprising in March, 1794, in a last-ditch effort to avert the absorption of Poland by Austria, Prussia and Russia. Beginning his movement in Krakow, Kościuszko deliberately appealed to the Jews, as well as to the Polish peasants, who had previously not been included in political life.

and particularly Jewish leaders, inclined towards loyalty to the authorities: all unrest could lead to violence against the Jews, and only the protection of the authorities offered any assurance of security and a stable life.

Roman Dmowski[7] stressed such Jewish loyalism and its incompatibility with Polish interests. There is also frequent mention of the "Litwak" issue—the Jews from the Russian interior who settled in the Congress Kingdom of Poland[8] in the late nineteenth century. Criticism of their Russifying influence misses the point that they lent dynamism to the Polish economy and enabled it to penetrate the internal Russian market. Their children, in any case, became Polonized. Finally, and this is the third point, the loyalist tendencies turned into support for the Polish state authorities after the recovery of independence. The conservative, Orthodox Aguda party supported each successive government in exchange for the preservation of broadly understood religious autonomy for the Jews. Furthermore, secondary and university education favoured the process of cultural Polonization in the second Republic. The fundamentally pro-state interests of the Jews were emphasized by some politicians from the camp aligned with Piłsudski. Dmowski's supporters, how-

7 Founder in 1893 of the National Democracy (*endecja*, *endek*) movement, Dmowski remained through the 1930s the ideologue of a narrowly nationalistic conception of the Polish state – as opposed to his great antagonist, Józef Piłsudski, who appealed to the expansionist, multi-ethnic traditions of the Polish-Lithuanian "Commonwealth" (which experienced its golden age in the sixteenth century). Both men made great contributions to the recovery of Polish independence at the end of the First World War. Perhaps fortuitously, it was Piłsudski who was hailed as the father of the Second Polish Republic. (After leading the 1926 coup against parliamentary government, Piłsudski ran the country from behind the scenes until his death in 1935; he and especially the "Colonels" who governed afterwards seemed in practice to pursue policies quite similar to those advocated by Dmowski.) The view that the Jews pose an economic and political threat to the Polish state has persistently been associated with Dmowski's views and the "Endecja" became virulently antisemitic before the Second World War.

8 The part of the Polish lands, including Warsaw, which was under Russian rule until the First World War. In 1795, Poland was partitioned into Russian, Prussian and Austrian parts.

ever, attacked the Jews even more vociferously than before – now, they regarded precisely their Polonization as dangerous. Given such an approach, nothing that the Jews could have done would have been satisfactory. This is just the place where antisemitism becomes apparent: loyalism and submission to the dominant culture are highlighted to the degree that they can be treated as accusations, and passed over in silence where they deserve praise.

The dilemmas of loyalism are well illustrated by the incidents in Lwów in 1918.[9] The Jews, fearing that support for either side would provoke reprisals from the other, decided to remain neutral while the Poles and the Ukrainians fought for the city. A Jewish militia guarded municipal institutions and food shops that served the whole population, and defended the Jews against looting. The looters included convicts who had been released from prison in order to join the defense of the city. Reports that Jews had fired on Polish defenders of Lwów became the impulse for a brutal pogrom on the day that a Polish relief force took possession of Lwów. The Polish command delayed taking countermeasures while Polish civilians and soldiers burned, looted and profaned the synagogues. More than a score of people died and many more were wounded. In Polish memory, this episode is an unfamiliar footnote to the joyous and almost legendary image of the victorious taking of the city, which had previously been heroically defended by the "fledgling eagles of Lwów." The pogrom is explained as a reprisal against the Jews for supporting the Ukrainians. Some authors still repeat this version today. It is inaccurate, although some Zionist groupings did in fact support Ukrainian aspirations,[10] on the principle that they

[9] Lwów or Lemberg, the capital of the Austro-Hungarian province of Galicia and Lodomeria until 1918; included in the Soviet Union after World War II; now the city of Lviv in independent Ukraine. Long an important Jewish cultural center, a cradle of Zionism from the 1880s onward, Lwów was until 1939 a Polish provincial capital, a city with a population approximately balanced among Polish, Jewish and Ukrainian communities, and the scene of fruitful inter-ethnic coexistence as well as tensions.

[10] Thus Jabotinsky features in recent Ukrainian historiography as a proponent of that country's statehood.

should be consistent in applying the principle that "everyone has the right to a separate national identity." What made the pogrom possible was the potential, destructive anti-Jewish energy that already existed previously.

Few Poles know today about the atmosphere engendered before the war by that hatred propagated against the Jews and the efforts made to complicate their lives, limit their opportunities, and simply push them out of the country. Jews remember that atmosphere all too well; too well because it fosters a one-sided, negative image, especially among people who do not know the real Poland. It is, nevertheless, true that antisemitism was a widely accepted political platform in Poland before the war. Otherwise respectable politicians and journalists planned ways of limiting Jewish rights or abolishing those rights altogether. "Aryan clauses" were adopted by many associations, and the emigration of the Jews was proposed as a remedy for unemployment. In January, 1939, 117 parliamentary delegates from the OZN (National Unification Camp, or the ruling party) tabled a motion on "radically reducing the number of Jews in Poland" as a way of "Polonizing" commerce. They also proposed "eliminating Jewish influences from Polish cultural and community life." In response, the prime minister stated that "the proposition that Jewish emigration from Poland should be intensified is advanced in unison by all of Polish public opinion." In the meantime, while the pressure on and readiness of Jews to emigrate increased, their actual opportunities for doing so dwindled. There was not the slightest support in Western Europe or the Western hemisphere for admitting larger numbers of Jews; in Palestine, the British introduced even more stringent limitations. The slogan "Jews to Madagascar," once heard in Poland, was as unrealistic as it was insulting. It deepened the frustration and encouraged Jews to think that no-one wanted them.

4. The War

Wartime produced remarkably divergent stereotypes among Poles on the one hand, and Jews around the world on the other. Everyone knows that it was hell for the Jews. The dominant Polish opinion, however, holds that it was likewise hell for the Poles, and furthermore that Poles sympathized with the Jews being murdered by the invader and offered as much help as they could, often sacrificing their lives in the process. The dominant opinion among Jews, on the other hand, is that the Poles greeted the murder of the Jews with approval, and sometimes joined in.

Each of these opinions is extraordinarily one-sided, even though a plethora of examples can be adduced in support of each. Everyone who has the slightest concept of what went on during the war understands the magnitude of Polish losses.[11] Outside Poland, however, most people remain unaware that the Germans assigned the Poles to the role of slaves whose culture was to be destroyed. Not even full knowledge about the fate of the Poles, however, can change the fact that, from the point of view of the burning Warsaw ghetto, life on the other side of the wall seemed incredibly normal. Shops and restaurants were opened and a merry-go-round[12] even operated: paradise next door to hell. It is, nonetheless, also a fact that Krakow seemed indecently normal to the inhabitants of Warsaw during the

[11] According to estimates up to three million non-Jewish Poles (a tenth of the population) died, many of whom in camps or in exile as a result of German and Soviet repression and persecutions; almost forty percent of the country's economic base was destroyed.

[12] The merry-go-round on Krasiński Square, noted in many memoirs, provided a powerful symbol in the wartime poem "Campo di Fiori," by the 1980 Nobel Prize laureate Czesław Miłosz. In turn, the literary scholar Jan Błoński used Miłosz's poem as the starting point for a 1987 essay in the Catholic intellectual weekly *Tygodnik Powszechny* on the question of the degree to which witnesses and bystanders bear guilt for the Shoah. A lively public debate ensued, on a Polish and international scale. Błonski's articles on the subject were collected in a volume bearing the same title as the original essay, "Biedni Polacy patrzą na getto" (Poor Poles Look at the Ghetto, Krakow, 1994).

1944 Uprising[13] in the capital – or that life in the ghetto seemed indecently normal to those who managed to escape from the first transports to Treblinka. It is therefore inaccurate to identify the dichotomy "tragedy-normalcy" with the dichotomy "Jews-Poles." Nevertheless, it is still false to equate Jewish and Polish fates. The Poles were decimated, while the great majority of Jews from Poland were murdered. What is more, only the Jews died without any reason apart from who they were. Only Jewish children were automatically doomed. It was for the Jews that the Nazis built the death camps.[14] These may seem

[13] The Warsaw Uprising began on the orders of the Polish Underground on August 1, 1944, as the Red Army raced westward towards the occupied Polish capital. The intention had been to wrest control from the Germans just before the entry of the Soviets. The Red Army halted east of the city and waited on the opposite bank of the Vistula, not crossing the river in force until the beginning of the final drive to Berlin in January, 1945. The insurgents succeeded in gaining initial control over large areas of the city; the Soviets and Poland's other allies did practically nothing; the Germans had a free hand systematically to assault, bomb, and burn the city until the last insurgents surrendered on September 10. During those six weeks, the Germans suffered considerable casualties while killing 22,000 Polish combatants and more than 100,000 civilians; the rest of the population driven from the city, which was left practically uninhabited, with 80% of its buildings destroyed, when the Soviets finally entered unopposed. The 1944 Uprising is routinely, and inexcusably, confused with the much smaller 1943 Ghetto Uprising by many foreigners, including visiting German presidents.

[14] The German concentration camps were based on the principle of working the prisoners to death in an effort to extract some economic advantage. Concentration camp prisoners were routinely shot and some concentration camps, most notably Auschwitz, had gas chambers where Jewish prisoners were killed immediately upon arrival. Even among the Jewish transports to Auschwitz, however, it was common for the Germans to "select" a proportion of the arrivals to be worked to death. (See also, Chapter 1 above). The death camps – Chełmno, Bełżec, Sobibor and Treblinka, form a distinct category. They had no labor function; they consisted only of crematoria and burial pits. No prisoners were selected for labor (except small bands employed in the manual labor of genocide, who were systematically killed off and replaced). While the concentration camps contained prisoners from nearly every ethnic group in Europe, the death camps were reserved for the killing of Jews. Built as part of "Operation Reinhard," these camps operated in 1942 and 1943. This is where most of the Jewish population of Poland died. When Operation Reinhard concluded, the camps were demolished and an effort made to obliterate all trace of them. Only a few prisoners survived; a group succeeded in escaping from Sobibor after a mutiny; apparently only two inmates survived Bełżec. Otherwise, there were no survivors.

like obvious truths, yet Poles sometimes deny them as if fearing that their own sufferings might be diminished. This leads to the phenomenon that Henryk Grynberg has called the "theft of the Holocaust": Jews killed for being Jews have their deaths appropriated. Along the way, victims are posthumously declared to have been Polish even if, during their lifetimes, any claims they made to that status were loudly shouted down.

The attitudes of Poles to Jews during the war were hardly uniform. Kindness and a desire to offer help appeared even among prewar antisemites, especially priests. The Church offered no official declarations. Many religious communities, especially female ones, nevertheless sheltered "non-Aryans." Orphanages run by nuns harboured Jewish children. The Jews in hiding often needed help. The aid offered either by individuals or by the organizations that made up the *Żegota* Jewish Aid Council (connected to the London government-in-exile) therefore had immense significance: it gave them a chance to survive. Such a chance was always minimal. Helping was not easy. Fugitives from the ghettos or the transports sometimes had no alternative to going back to the ghetto. Some tried to survive in the forests. This was not easy, especially since partisan units tended not to accept Jews. Even in cities, it was quite difficult for Jews to join the Home Army resistance movement.[15] This was not official policy from headquarters. Rather, it reflected either mistrust or awareness that, in the underground, Jews were a foreign element with a fate of their own. Going into hiding was unimaginably difficult, despite the fact that there were people ready to help at the right price, and others good enough never to mention money. They, however, were not the ones who defined the atmosphere in which

[15] The largest armed Polish resistance movement, formally established under the London government-in-exile in 1942, operating on a nationwide scale with a Supreme Commander in Poland. All legitimate Polish underground soldiers were part of the Home Army (or AK), except for the communist People's Guard (later, People's Army) and the extreme right-wing National Armed Forces (later, partially incorporated into the AK).

Jews hid. The Jews were terrorized by "bounty hunters," blackmailers who extorted money under threat of informing the Gestapo. According to recent research, blackmail became the source of income, a usual business of that period, for thousands of mostly normal Poles. Fugitives from the ghetto could die at the hands of these blackmailers, or at the hands of partisans or bandits who saw them as easy pickings.

Poles in general, of course, took no part in the killing. On the other hand, it is not possible to say that Poles in general offered aid to the Jews. There is nothing strange about this in view of how hard it was to do so in the circumstances of terror under German occupation—or how risky it was. Each act of aid was punishable by death. Those who lost their lives in this way deserve to be remembered with all the more gratitude. It can be said that the help was not forgotten: trees are planted in honour of the "righteous among the nations" at Yad Vashem in Jerusalem. Among 20757 so honoured, 5874 Poles constitute the largest group. Many more, however, remain unknown.

I am sure that the world knows too little about Polish help to Jews. One of the reasons is that Poles themselves have not been keen to learn the facts. It is amazing that in Poland until recently almost nothing was known about two Polish heroes who rescued Jews during World War II. Ms. Irena Sendler worked for the health department of the city of Warsaw and was among the few Christians allowed to enter the ghetto. She helped to smuggle 2500 Jewish children out of the ghetto and place them in hiding. Many of them survived, either in private homes or in convents and monasteries. On a similar scale was the action of a Polish diplomat Henryk Sławik, sometimes called "the Polish Wallenberg". He served in Budapest when Hungary was still semi-independent, and there he help provide false "Aryan" documents to several thousand Polish Jews who were then in Hungary. This enabled them to pass and avoid the transports to Auschwitz organized by the Fascist Hungary. When the Germans occupied Hungary in 1944, Sławik was arrested and killed in Mauthausen. Despite torture he did not disclose his collaborators. A few years ago, Shevach Weiss, the former speaker of the Knesset and the Israeli ambassador to Poland, said that if Poland had had better PR, Raoul Wallenberg would have been called "the Swedish Sławik."

The German terror unquestionably justified passivity. However, it did not rule out sympathy. Sympathy, nevertheless, was not at all the rule. Time after time, Jews in hiding confronted indifference stemming from the assumption: "the war between the Jews and the Germans does not concern us." They met with unfriendliness, and at times also with expressions of satisfaction about the one good thing that Hitler was doing—he was freeing Poland of the Jews. The heroic aid extended to Jews by Poles took place not only in opposition to the Germans. The fact that it took place in opposition to other Poles was one of the reasons that it was so difficult and risky. It is a fact that, even after the war, some people feared to admit that they had helped the Jews. When Michał Borwicz began collecting and publishing accounts of aid, in which he gave the names of the benefactors, some of them began complaining that they had encountered "unpleasantness," and in some cases even "reprisals." This attests to the atmosphere of those times. Poles today have no idea of what it was like. Yet that atmosphere was the source of the experiences that serve as a pretext for antipolonism.

The controversy over blame and merit is, to a large degree, a controversy over who represents Poland – the noblest, the basest, or the average people? The Polish government-in-exile in London conveyed information and acted as intermediary in passing money from the West to the ghettos. It sounded the alarm, and the world did nothing. These are indisputable merits. It is true, however, that the government-in-exile's statements to the Allies sounded different from its statements to the domestic Polish population. When Sikorski[16] proclaimed during a 1942 meeting in London that Jews would receive equal rights after the war, such remarks were edited out of a radio broadcast to Poland. The death sentences passed against "bounty hunters" indicate the attitude of the Home Army leadership. At the same time, Jewish resistance activists felt that the leaders of Underground Poland did not feel responsible for their Jewish citizens. Their operational plans did not take them into account and there were no Jewish representatives in the clandestine domestic leadership (as opposed to the London government).

5. After the War

The war changed the situation, but it brought no radical change to attitudes towards Jews. The image of Jews as not only alien and harmful, but as downright hostile, remained in place. Attitudes towards Jews outlived the Jews themselves, as shown by a statement in "*Walka*" (The Fight) an underground right-wing newspaper from July, 1943 – after the liquidation of most Jewish population centres and after the Warsaw Ghetto Uprising. Stating that the percentage of Jews in the Polish population had been reduced to the level of the percentage of Jews in Germany before the war, the author averred that "we regard the Jewish question as almost resolved. When Jewish capital and Jewish intrigues took control of Germany after the last war, the problem was not viewed with complacency!" Of course, other newspapers wrote differently. The socialist and communist newspapers stressed the importance of community. The moderate clandestine press, like the official Home Army's "*Biuletyn Informacyjny*" (Information Bulletin), presented the fate of the Jews hon-

[16] General Władysław Sikorski, head of the Polish government-in-exile in London, died in a plane crash off Gibraltar on July 4, 1943.

estly and with sympathy. Some pre-war antisemites now aided Jews. This was not, however, the rule. Voices such as that quoted above were not isolated. Yet they did not indicate any participation in the destruction. While the Holocaust may not have transformed Polish thinking about the Jews, nevertheless, Polish antisemitism had nothing in common with the Nazi campaign to murder all Jews. I believe that the German extermination machine would have done its work even if all Poles had loved Jews.

For Polish pride, perhaps the most difficult to understand and accept is the fact of the murder of Jewish inhabitants of Jedwabne and several other Polish towns by their neighbours in 1941. This happened in formerly Soviet-occupied areas, immediately after the German conquest. It was done under German supervision but without direct German participation; the pretext used was the presence of Jews in the Soviet ruling apparatus, responsible for repression and deportations. Yet, Jews were among both those who were deported and those organising the deportations. The large-scale pogroms were by no means unique to Poland. They were stimulated by German occupiers in many Eastern countries, often on a much larger scale. In Poland, as elsewhere, for decades the events were never discussed. And only in Poland, since 2000, has a very serious discussion resulted. Everywhere, in occupied Poland Polish Christians witnessed the murder of Jews. In most places they got used to it. Some provided help to the occupiers. In a few places the Christian neighbours killed by themselves. This does pose a very serious moral challenge. This challenge is recognized nowadays by perhaps half of Poles. The fact remains, though, that the numbers of Jews killed is just a minute fraction of those murdered by the Nazi Germany death machinery. Let me repeat that even if all Poles had loved Jews in the reality of that time the result would have been largely the same. A few hundred thousand more Jews would have survived but millions would have been murdered anyway. The opposite opinion is more frequently held by Jews who are incapable of believing that the situation was hopeless, and who draw, from Polish attitudes to Jews before and immediately after the war, conclusions that are too far-reaching.

War-time murders of Jews were committed by Lithuanians, Ukrainians, Hungarians, Romanians, and others. The fact that Jews were killed in Poland in the years 1945–1946 had almost no parallel in Europe. One factor was the struggle against "Jewish communism."[17] More than one underground unit treated Jews and communists as identical. Obviously, Jews were not the only ones to be shot at, and many people lost their lives and freedom. Seldom do people in the West know anything about this. Another danger factor for Jewish survivors was the fact that the people who had taken over Jewish homes and businesses had no intention of giving them up. As early as 1943, a report from circles associated with the government-in-exile's Delegation[18] in Poland recommended that the emigration of the surviving Jews be carried out after the war because the population would treat the return of the Jews to their homes as an "invasion." The post-war danger to the Jews resulted from many sources. During the bloodiest of the pogroms, which claimed 42 dead and many injured in Kielce, in July 1946, police and soldiers from the Polish People's Army were active among the crowd.

The last anti-Jewish campaign in Poland to be organized officially and on a large scale was the one that reached its peak in March,

[17] Even in the nineteenth century, Jews were associated in Polish literature with revolution and anarchy. The myth of "Jewish communism" ("*Żydokomuna*", a repulsively pejorative term in Polish, somewhat like "Jewcommies") fueled by the Russian Revolution and the 1920 Polish-Soviet War, holds that communism (illogically said to be supported by Jewish financiers), is simply a part of the world-wide (and invariably "anti-Polish") "Jewish conspiracy".

[18] The *Delegatura*, under the leadership of a Plenipotentiary appointed from the government-in-exile in London, was in effect the civil administrative arm of the Polish Underground State; it had a central bureaucracy and a local structure down to the municipal level.

1968.[19] Even Jews who were completely Polonized, as well as people suspected of Jewish origins, were dismissed from their jobs and harassed in order to encourage them to emigrate. This campaign was organized at the highest levels of authority and was part of an intra-party power struggle. It did not originate at the grass-roots level. For outside observers, however, it cast a shadow on the image of Poland. Its nature and dimensions remain unique in post-war Europe.

The struggle against "Jewish communism" is a characteristic theme on the Polish political scene. It was there before the war and during the war. It was present in a certain sense after the war, and it is still warmed up from time to time even now. The accusations intensified in the years 1939–1941 as a result of the participation by Jews in the authorities created in the Polish eastern lands after they were seized by the Red Army. It is a fact that many Jews, like other minorities in the same territories, spent little time mourning the passing of a Polish state in which they felt like second-class

[19] In a complex intra-Party factional dispute in the late 1960s, a "Partisan" clique of former communist Resistance fighters and an ambitious group of younger apparatchiks combined to attack the entrenched party establishment, many of whom were of Jewish origin. The Soviet-led diplomatic offensive against Israel after the Six-Day War provided the pretext for using "anti-Zionism" as the key slogan when this local Polish purge (used instead of a non-existing election mechanism) broke out in March, 1968 (in an atmosphere made tense by student protests and Dubcek's short-lived reforms in neighboring Czechoslovakia). At the time and for many years later, few Poles outside the Party elite knew (or cared, probably) about the real issues. Nevertheless, an "anti-Zionist" campaign filled the media, including speeches by First Secretary Gomułka to factory audiences obediently holding the appropriate signs and banners. Right down to the grass-roots, party-cell level, "Zionists" were publicly denounced and expelled, and the press enthusiastically published the details. Excluding mistakes and exceptions, only Jews, of course, could be accused of "Zionism," and every Jew was accused. The obsession spread to the arts, publishing, and industrial management; in effect, every professionally active person of Jewish origin was pressured to leave the country. Considering the atmosphere, many did so enthusiastically; others left under duress. As in the case of the Kielce Pogrom of 1946, the world could only wonder how such a thing could happen in post-Shoah Europe. As Rafael Scharf has remarked, the most telling thing is that, for all those years, tabs were kept on exactly who was of Jewish descent.

citizens. They looked on the change in power with a certain hope, and in some cases with enthusiasm – positions that they could never have dreamed about in Poland, in administration or the military, for instance, now became accessible to them. For Poles, this was treason. Yet Polish public opinion was blind to the fact that there were Jewish politicians, like the Bund leaders Henryk Ehrlich and Wiktor Alter,[20] who remained entirely loyal to the vanquished Polish state. Furthermore, Jews shared the woes of the time: they constituted 30% of the Polish citizens deported eastward into the Russian interior. Some Jews were happy to be out of Hitler's reach. Yet it is also a fact of which Poles are unaware that thousands of Jews refused to accept Soviet passports early in the war and asked permission to return to the territory occupied by the Germans. Many such people were deported eastward rather than being allowed to travel west. The journey east, although undertaken against their will, saved their lives. It might be said that deportation was fortunate for them – a paradox that did not form part of the Polish experience. Poles still argue today over which occupation was worse, German or Soviet. For Jews, the question is not open to discussion.

Once the war had ended, the accusation about "Jewish communism" took on substance as a result of the widespread participation by Jews in the newly-created system of rule that had been imposed on the country. Polish public opinion failed to note two key facts. First, the majority of the Jews, whether they had survived in Poland or returned from the Soviet Union, tried to leave Poland as quickly as possible. Second, the reasons that people joined the communists had nothing to do with their origins. Jews did not participate in authority as a group, but rather as individuals, and not as Jews, but as communists. During the Stalinist period, the Jews were subject to the same restrictions as

[20] These anti-communist leaders of the Bund, or Jewish Socialist Party, the most powerful Jewish political group before the war, were members of the Socialist International executive. They were killed by the Soviet NKVD in December, 1941, although the Soviets refused until 1943 to reveal their fate.

everyone else. No anti-communist Jewish institutions had any hope of surviving. Stalin's antisemitism was well known in the West and provided the viewpoint from which Poland was observed. The concept of "Jewish secret policeman" became a symbol that was widely current in Polish public opinion; the West is rather more familiar with the Kielce pogrom.

From the start, there was no shortage of Jewish victims of communist oppression. However, this did not determine the atmosphere in Poland; rather, the populace remembered the frequency with which they encountered Jewish officers, party confidants, and fanatical Marxists. Such people usually did not want to be Jewish. They tried to keep their distance from Jewish organizations and Jewish concerns. As a rule, they opted for total assimilation and the rejection of the distinction between Jews and Poles. They were often Polonized, and even more often attempted to conceal their origins. This made them all the more conspicuous.

Can the argument about "Jews in the UB"[21] be used against Jews, including those from the West? Today's Poles have had a taste of such accusations. In the 1990s, the Polish minority in Lithuania was often unenthusiastic about Lithuanian independence, and some Polish leaders there proposed a Polish autonomous region connected with Moscow. How can Poles be pro-Soviet? Such behaviour results not from their nature, but rather from their situation as a minority and their fear of the triumphant nationalism of the majority.

[21] The UB (*Urząd Bezpieczeństwa* – the Security Bureau) was the communist political police in the Stalinist period (1944–1956). It used methods of terror and provocation in an effort to crush non-communist and anti-communist social structures, including the Catholic Church. In the immediate aftermath of the Soviet occupation of Poland (1944–1945), the UB functioned openly as an auxiliary to the Soviet Secret Police.

6. Acceptance

Although less known around the world, pro-Jewish attitudes have always been present in Poland. For many generations, Jews were accepted as a natural ingredient in the country, different but familiar, fulfilling necessary functions. Modern nationalism, however, emphasized that the presence of Jews is harmful. Stressing their differences with the Jews was one way of awakening the national consciousness of the common people. The identification of Poles with Catholicism was intended to lead to national purity. Piłsudski and his followers, with their vision of a multi-ethnic Poland as a successor to the Polish state that had been wiped off the map in the eighteenth century, represented a different approach. Piłsudski himself had no time for antisemitism, and the right wing accused his governments of excessive liberalism towards the Jews. It is a fact that, despite increasing emigration, the majority of Jews saw their future in Poland. While the Zionists advocated emigration, they were opposed by both the Orthodox traditionalists and the Socialists in the Bund, and thus by the majority. In 1928, the Yiddish author Szalom Asz wrote, "Fate has linked us to the Polish nation for eternity." Some Jews from Poland were proud of their Polishness. One example is Artur Rubinstein, the famous pianist. Many Poles are also proud of such Jews and their accomplishments.

There is universal recognition in Poland of the Jewish contribution, by artists, writers, scientists and industrialists, to the country's culture. The pithy remark attributed to a pre-World War II provincial governor of Lwów reflects this: "Jews? Emigrate? Hell, stay here and make Polish culture!" The presence of traditional Jews, with their customs, folklore and cooking, gave Polish life an additional dimension. That world has passed irrevocably into history. Some Poles do not even know the source of the *challah* bread, matzo or "Jewish-style carp." Many others sense how the country has been impoverished. As the poet Zbigniew Herbert put it, "Poland without Jews (and other minorities) is not Poland."

That bygone Poland sometimes crops up in unexpected places. The folk image of the Jew combines such negative traits as dirtiness and collusion with the devil, with positive ones like wisdom and healing powers. It was not only Jews who sought the advice of the *tzaddik*, the charismatic Hasidic leader, the Rebbe. Long after the war, non-Jews were still going to the grave of a *tzaddik*, in some abandoned or even devastated cemetery, to ask for intercession.

Jewish culture reached its greatest development among the landscapes, folklore and even the historical events of old Poland, and that culture is therefore Polish in a certain sense. This is best illustrated by Stanisław Vincenz,[22] who recorded that world of rich complexity. A Hasid told him how he was studying Russian and Polish literature: Russian literature is Dostoyevsky and Tolstoy, human affairs, while Polish literature is religious affairs: the Great Magid, the words of the Baal Shem-Tov, Mendel of Witebsk, Nachman of Bratslav and the others. Through the legacy of such writers, something of old Poland survives today in the wider world.

Polish consciousness contains instances where Polish-Jewish cooperation took on a form so profound that it has become symbolic: Berek Joselewicz formed Jewish units that fought in Kościuszko's 1794 Uprising; Michał Landy took the cross from a wounded Catholic during an anti-Tsarist demonstration in 1861 and was himself shot dead; Ber Meisels, as chief rabbi of Warsaw, supported actions against the Russian partitioning power.[23] Meisels even

[22] Author of epic, quasi-mythical accounts of the multi-ethnic world of his homeland in the Eastern Carpathians (now Ukraine), an area associated with the rise of the Hasidim, many of whose tales Vincenz collected. After World War II, he lived near the Alps.

[23] Particularly among those who favored cultural assimilation or proclaimed themselves "Poles of Jewish origin" or "Poles of the Mosaic faith," these historical figures were, before the war, icons of Jewish commitment to Polish independence, and therefore of Jewish loyalty to the Polish state.

remarked in a sermon that Moses Isserles, the great Talmudic authority and sixteenth-century rabbi of Krakow, "indicated to us that we should love the Polish nation above all other nations, for the Poles have been our brothers for centuries." This is striking testimony to a pro-Polish attitude that contemporary Jews may find unimaginable.

Jankiel, in Adam Mickiewicz's epic poem "Pan Tadeusz"[24], is an extraordinary figure who may have no parallel in other literatures. This "honest Jew," who "loved Poland like a Pole," is a mainstay of patriotism. And this is hardly the only example of Mickiewicz's philosemitism. His idea of forming a "Jewish Legion" may have led nowhere, but his injunction to honour and accord equal rights to "Israel, the older brother" set an important pro-Jewish precedent. Even when the tide later turned, Mickiewicz remained such an important architect of the Polish national vision that his precepts retained some currency. People unfamiliar with Polish culture and the role that the poet-prophet plays in it can have no idea of his importance. Every Polish child learns about Jankiel.

Jankiel was a traditional Jew. The nineteenth century brought assimilation and the appearance of new types of Jews, and thus of Poles. The novelist Józef Ignacy Kraszewski wrote to his father that the financier Leopold Kronenberg,[25] recently baptized, "is no worse a Pole than we are." Polonization may be treated as testimony to the attractiveness of Polish culture, and this helps account for the sympathy shown by Polish intellectuals. Assimilation found disfavour, however, among followers of the Jewish national movements. It was not always accompanied by baptism. In the first census held in independent Poland, in 1922, one-fourth of the people who were Jewish by religious denomination declared themselves to be of Polish nationality.

[24] One of the main works by Adam Mickiewicz (1798-1855), the foremost Polish Romantic poet, and still a major influence on Polish culture.

[25] An industrialist, financier and philanthropist, Leopold Kronenberg (1812–1878) provided substantial funding for the 1863 Uprising.

7. Opportunities

Is a Poland without antisemitism possible? Can good Polish-Jewish relations be achieved? There can be no doubt that relations with Jews have always rather divided than united Poles. The affirmation of Polishness need not be connected with antisemitism, just as the affirmation of Jewishness need not involve an aversion to Poland. It remains a fact that, while some Poles have always been friendly to Jews, they have seldom set the prevailing tone.

True Polish-Jewish contacts belong to the past. With the possible exception of the problem of the restitution of property, which involves nothing specifically Jewish, there are no longer any real Polish-Jewish conflicts, only controversies over symbols and the interpretation of the past. The controversy over the convent at Auschwitz could be perceived as another exception.[26] Yet it, too, was concerned with the sphere of symbols. Around the world, Auschwitz has become a symbol of the destruction of the Jews; in Poland, it is also a symbol of the sufferings of the Poles. The controversy represented an opportunity for the two sides to understand each other better. So far, however – apart from numerous exceptions on both sides – a lack of understanding is dominant. The Jews wanted Poles to acknowledge their guilt towards the Jews. The Poles wanted Jews to stop treating Poland as an antisemitic nation and admit that they had reasons for gratitude to the Poles.

To give an example, the negative stereotype can be detected in the relatively widespread use of the phrase "Polish concentration camp" by the Western media. While it often refers to the geographical location, the adjective "Polish" suggests Polish guilt. In many countries Polish complicity has become an obvious association. This is unjust, even though Poles have not passed the test with which the Holocaust faced the nation. However, despite the anti-Jewish

[26] For more details, see above Chapter 1, 3.1.

attitudes and activities of many Polish Christians, Poles were only among the inmates of Nazi camps, which were planned and run by Germans and Austrians, with many Ukrainian guards, never Polish ones. That is why the phrase "Polish camps" is offensive to us, especially in view of the virtual lack of the proper attribution of the creators and managers of the Nazi camps, the Germans. The proper phrase in connection with Auschwitz and other death camps may be "Nazi-German camp in Poland" or "Nazi camp in German-occupied Poland". This point was forcefully made in a public statement of the American Jewish Committee (AJC), released in February 2005 by its executive director, David Harris. I am glad that in this way a major American Jewish organization has joined the efforts of Polish institutions.

The above example is an exception rather than the rule. The less understanding from the other side, the greater the wall dividing "insensitive Poles" from "ungrateful Jews"; can that wall ever be torn down?

Among the Polish intelligentsia, there has been growing interest for more than two decades in Jewish culture, the history of the Jews in Poland, and Judaism. The sources run deep. First, it is an effort to reach all the wellsprings of Polishness. Second, it results from a reorientation of Church teachings, which now acknowledge the permanent values of Jews and Judaism. Some religious young Poles go even further than the official Church position. They regard it as obvious that no attempt should be made to convert Jews; that Jews should be Jews in a religious sense. There is also some interest in the state of Israel, which has overturned many of the old stereotypes about Jews. There are as well more and more valuable attempts at Christian-Jewish dialogue in Poland[27], although the numerical disproportion between the two faiths is greater in Poland than in other countries active in the dialogue. Polish historians are coop-

[27] See Chapters 7 and 8 below.

erating with their Western and Israeli colleagues in studying the history of the Jews in Poland. To mention another recent initiative, the Forum for Dialogue among Nations has been running exchange programs of Polish and American Jewish groups, with the help of the Ministry of Foreign Affairs of Poland, and in partnership with the American Jewish Committee. All these efforts have an elitist nature, although it is the elite which finally shapes popular thinking.

The elites, however, are not unanimous. Respect for Judaism may be taught in one church while the notorious antisemitic forgery "The Protocols of the Elders of Zion" is sold in another; one church may preach tolerance while another enjoins the faithful to vote only for "true Poles." Poets shape the way Poles think, but Mickiewicz, Norwid[28] and Miłosz are not the only poets. For the majority of Poles, the image of the Jews is symbolized not so much by Jankiel as by the sinister figure of Pankracy, the "convert" who leads a destructive revolution in Krasiński's "Un-Divine Comedy"[29].

The most important factor is the atmosphere created by the public authorities and the silent majority. The pro-Nazi graffiti on the walls of Polish cities or the broken windows in Jewish institutions are the work of a minority. Yet they will remain an accepted, "normal" part of Polish life unless they are loudly condemned by the authorities, the Church, moral authorities and passers-by.

For a long time, criticism of traditional antisemitism in postwar Poland was difficult. Not all truths could be spoken aloud; taboos prevailed in the history of Polish antisemitic attitudes of the 1940s. Public criticism of communist antisemitism was practically unthinkable until the rise of "Solidarity," which also represented a turning point in the discussion of Jewish affairs. Then, however, it also turned out that the post–1968 emigration of most of the Jews or people of Jewish origin had not eliminated the false charge that the

[28] Cyprian Norwid, an important nineteenth-century Polish poet who lived in Paris, and became well- known only in the twentieth century.

[29] This is another major literary work of an important nineteenth-century Romantic poet.

high number of Jews in the country lay behind unpopular attitudes, distortions of the truth and hostile acts.

Too many Jews? Before the war, the finger was pointed at a minority of more than three million, and at the role of Jews in the economy and culture. Even those who held that the Jews made a positive contribution had to admit that those three million were indeed present in Poland. After the war there were only a few hundred thousand to point at, and most of them were in the process of emigrating. Yet the Jewish communists were still there, occupying high posts in the power structure, including the secret police. Even those who believed that they were acting as communists and not as Jews had to admit that they were indeed present. Later, in the 1960s, the Party pointed the finger at the Marxist revisionists of Jewish descent and their children among the rebellious students. Even those who, like the majority of the intelligentsia, held that those revisionists were working for the good of the country and that it was better for Stalinists to become anti-Stalinists than vice-versa, still had to admit that they were indeed present. Later, the finger was pointed at KOR[30] and at the advisers to "Solidarity." After 1981, it was pointed at the Rakowski government and the anti-communist political underground. Then it was pointed at the Mazowiecki government, and serious politicians warned that if the government adopted policies unfavourable to peasants, "then we will have antisemitism." Finally, it was pointed at President Kwaśniewski and other pro-European Union politicians. There has always been someone to point the finger at!

According to surveys made in 1992 and 2002[31], asked the question about the number of Jews in Poland, 27% in 2002 (23% in 1992)

[30] "*Komitet Obrony Robotników*"—the Committee for the Defense of the Workers, the first overt structure of the Polish democratic opposition, was founded after the 1976 suppression by the communist authorities of striking industrial workers. Its activists have been active, and in some cases prominent, in Polish politics since 1989.

[31] Data taken from: Ireneusz Krzemiński (ed.) *Antysemityzm w Polsce i na Ukrainie*, Wydawnictwo Naukowe SCHOLAR, Warszawa 2004.

said "many", and 45% said "few" in 2002 (37% in 1992). Asked to check a number, 2.5% showed "several million" (!) (in 1992, 3.5%), and 9% "hundreds of thousands" (13.6% in 1992). And the real number is dozens of thousands.[32] All of this clearly shows that antisemites do not care about the number of Jews. Some sort of magical process occurs. The presence of Jews, real or imagined, is more important than the arguments. So it is when a mythical national purity and a closed, homogenous faith become the overriding goals. Explaining evil by way of Jewish influences is a sickness that endangers democracy. How can Poland ever attain normality?

Jews, who as a rule are now Jews only by reason of descent, are engaged on various sides in many conflicts. Yet antisemites only point the finger at their opponents. After 1989, the Star of David is added to many election posters in order to discredit the candidate. Similarly, the Jewishness of people accused of crimes is noted, like the head of a post-war camp where under the command of Solomon Morel – who has recently escaped to Israel – prisoners were tortured, not infrequently to death; or the crooks who escaped to Israel in the 1990s to avoid prosecution for fraud. On the other hand, it is difficult to imagine anyone publicly mentioning the Jews on his own side of the political barrier in a matter-of-fact way, let alone doing so with pride. Doing so would mean displeasing both the antisemites and the people who wish to conceal their own Jewish ancestors. Yet why not do so? Only when this becomes conceivable and ultimately natural – not to say obligatory – will antisemitism have been vanquished.

[32] More about the difficult problem of establishing the number of Jews currently living in Poland is said in Chapter 6.

Poland And The Jews: Inescapable Issues

Abstract

Today's Polish Jews are overwhelmingly assimilated to Polish culture, but some have regained their ties to Jewishness. Ten more basic points describing the situation are to be kept in mind in discussions of relations between Poland and Jews in the world: World War II is the basic point of reference; Auschwitz is possibly the best-known place name in Poland; for foreign Jews Poland is primarily a cemetery; the Jedwabne massacre debate has broken all taboos and is going so deep that it can heal the memories; the experience of communism must not be ignored; Polish Romanticism is still important; no reconciliation is possible by mere reference to the "idyllic" co-existence up to the 18th century; the Holocaust is an important element of the universal, not just Polish, Christian-Jewish dialogue; the restitution of property is still an issue; the path to reconciliation between Poland and Jews will not be short and easy. The text was read in February 2002, in the Center of Jewish Culture in Krakow, directed by Dr. Joachim Russek, at a meeting hosted by Prof. Jan Woleński, to a Polish, mostly Christian, audience. A Polish version appeared in *Res Publica nowa* 7/2002.

I prefer to speak of *Poland and the Jews* rather than *Poles and Jews*, the latter threatening to limit my freedom of movement within the present subject-matter. *Poland and the Jews* leaves ample room for all Jews, including Polish Jews, Jews living in Poland and Jews who consider themselves Poles; *Poles and Jews*, on the other hand, suggests two separate categories, which in turn would force me to take sides and this, despite all my public commitment to Jewish affairs, is something I do not wish to do.

Incidentally, my interest in Jewish issues also has a *private* dimension – something by far not as self-evident as it may seem, there being enough people today who function as Jews in public but pursue nothing specifically Jewish in their private lives. I am far from contending this as it is their good right to feel this way, I am also sure such people are aware of their Jewish heritage and at least to some degree identify with other Jews and Jewish problems – and the fate of the Jewish people. Their lives, however, differ in no way from those of their non-Jewish peers. This situation is best described by turning around one of the French Revolution's popular slogans, namely that one should be "Jewish at home and French in public". Similarly, we sometimes encounter people who are Jews in public and "French" (Polish) in private. In this connection I have to say that I not only feel ties with the Jews and (some of) their problems, but also put on my *tefillin* each morning and pray, as well as observing several other "specifically Jewish" rites.

As for terminology, however, even I feel uneasy when I am described as a Jew and not a Pole. Of course I am Jewish, but equally evidently – at least for myself – I am Polish. I am aware that some Poles do not accept this. Neither do some Jews. It is, however, a fact that the vast majority of today's Polish Jews belong to both categories, with many among the younger generation – and some of the elders too – tending to unawareness of their Jewish heritage. Some again may ambitiously deny their double nationality, not wanting to "beg" for the right to be Polish. I know I don't; hence, when someone denies me this right I have no wish to argue – though I usually meet people who wouldn't even think of denying it.

I feel uneasy arguing about interpretations of the right to be Polish. I do, however, feel compelled to point out some facts. Most Jews in Poland today take their Polishness for granted. Not just because they know the language and the country's history, take part in Polish cultural life or feel tied to the Christian tradition (people declaring themselves both Jews and Catholics are a separate and interesting issue). For them Polishness is something that is "theirs" from the start, an environment in which they live and grow up. And this has nothing to do with the clamouring for Polishness typical of the latter half of the nineteenth and the first half of the twentieth centuries. Today the assimilation process is complete and in this respect Poland generally resembles the Western countries. However, some parts of society appear to be evolving in the opposite direction - and now aspire to their Jewishness.

Returning to Judaism was and still is a major challenge for an overwhelming majority of young Polish Jews and quite a few of those not so young, including myself. Historically, this is probably an unprecedented phenomenon, although similar problems were encountered by the descendants of the *maranos* emigrating from Spain 400 years ago. In any case, Polishness is the starting-point here. Polishness understood not as "awareness" or "a right" but as a fact. Of course some may claim that this is not true Polishness but feigned or fragmentary (for example, because it is not Catholic). I have no wish to argue this but I must stress once again: regardless of how "correct" or not it is, this Polishness is not pretended but real – and *this* is a *fact*.

Thus we come to our first – albeit not necessarily foremost – crucial issue (which, as it is somewhat marginal to our present theme, I will list as number zero).

0. Most Jews in today's Poland are Poles, although this was not always so

The above statement is descriptive and not a judgement (who knows whether the present situation is better or worse). Although the evolution towards gradual assimilation – or at least cultural adjustment – to Polishness began in the nineteenth century and intensified in the inter-war years, the true breakthrough in this respect came like greased lightning – mainly driven, of course, by the Holocaust. And this brings us to the second, and probably most important, crucial issue.

1. World War Two remains the main factor in Polish-Jewish relations

This is so obvious that it needs no further comment.

We are often at a loss to determine what Poland is known for in the world. Are there any names or product brands associated with Poland? Is it vodka? Or perhaps Polish sausages? Or *bigos*[1], or coal, or the Polish bison? None of these are universally recognizable names. What about famous people? The West rather associates Chopin and Maria Skłodowska-Curie with France, Copernicus with Germany (at least equally with Poland), Miłosz is known only to elites. Lech Wałęsa? True, there was a time when he was widely known (however strange this may seem from the present Polish perspective), but these days are past and will unavoidably become more distant. Pope John Paul II will certainly remain known as the head of the Catholic Church but I doubt that the average Japanese, Hindu or Brazilian really knows or cares that this Pope was Polish. Place names like Warsaw or Krakow? Europeans know them, but the Japanese?

1 *Bigos* – a traditional Polish stew made of sauerkraut, meat and mushrooms.

What then? Is anything Polish at all known in Japan, India or Brazil? I believe so. And it is something very close to our present theme.

2. The most famous Polish place name - and perhaps the name most associated with Poland – is Auschwitz

I am not saying this is right or just for Poland. Nonetheless, instead of feeling insulted it may be better for Poland to accept this as fact. Auschwitz exudes a huge, global symbolic force which properly applied could make it an important centre of European reflection. Itself a symbol of terror and death, it could be successfully constructed into a site for fundamental debate. Poland is extremely important from the Jewish historical perspective and the Shoah is such a fresh experience that it must dominate all thinking about Poland by foreign Jews.

3. In the eyes of non-Polish Jews Poland is a Jewish cemetery

This is understandable but alien to my thinking, as for me Poland is first and foremost the place where I live my daily life. Nonetheless, I am not surprised that foreigners mainly see absence, death and graveyards. The figures are undisputable: the years 1939–1943 saw a 90 percent fall in the Jewish population, with a further fall in subsequent years (just try to imagine this on a chart). It is enough to look around any Polish small town to sense the absence of Jews. Thus, although my friends and I often protest opinions that there are no Jews left in Poland, I am not surprised that foreigners see the Jewish absence more clearly than they see us.

The question that arises here for Poland is whether anyone is really sorry for the Shoah victims. Was Poland as a community ever in true mourning for the Jews? Does Poland suffer being – besides everything else – a Jewish cemetery? To me, the answer is obvious. Father Stanisław Musiał once said it with full force: "The Jews know we are pleased that Poland's Jewish problem has been resolved once and for all, and not by our hands at that."

Of course there are those who are truly sorry. However, appropriate steps need to be taken if such regrets are to be credible. They have to be spoken out loud; the populations of Polish towns and villages should take more interest in their localities' and their Jewish inhabitants' past, look after their Jewish cemeteries. Some do this, but these are exceptions not the rule.

Recent debates around the Jedwabne affair showed explicitly that the failure to regret such deeds may arise from a bad conscience. Everywhere, the disappearance of the town's Jewish population brought their neighbours certain advantages; in some places the neighbours lent a helping hand. This is something the Jews always knew one way or the other but which was a total taboo in Poland, with no one daring to take up the subject in public for fifty years – until Agnieszka Arnold's film and Jan T. Gross's book.

4. Jedwabne: possible starting-point of a healing debate

Polish debates on the history of Poland's Jews are permeated with the Polish innocence obsession (to use Joanna Tokarska-Bakir's term). This obsession lies at the core of a defensive stance which rejects not only all thought of guilt, but also all mention of shameful – or even merely dubious – events in the past. Until recently this attitude was predominant in Poland; today, however, the consensus behind its perseverance has been severely shaken.

The Jedwabne debate is magnificent and I feel proud that such a deep discussion was possible at all. There are no taboos any more today and the last few years have brought many penetrating and subtle analyses of the subject written by the above-mentioned

Father Musiał, Joanna Tokarska-Bakir, Anna Bikont, and others, not to mention the fundamental volumes of documents and research produced by the Institute of National Remembrance.

I would particularly like to mention one text, written not by a single author but by two staffers at the popular weekly *Wprost*: "Our Fault. Our Apology to the Jews and Plea for Forgiveness" by Stanisław Janecki and Jerzy Sławomir Mac[2]. The authors mention ten sins: silence, indifference, greed, cowardice, ingratitude, rejection, official antisemitism, guilt, Zionism obsessions, and doorstep antisemitism. They also apologise for all whom, as they put it, "have no wish to apologise for all this". The article, which cuts right through the Poles' defensiveness on the issue, moved me deeply. It shows an understanding of the Jewish experience in Poland, and opens up human hearts. And it is at such times that I want to shout out: yes, of course I forgive you, my brothers. I know you had nothing to do with this evil. Paradoxically, one may well ask *how* I know this. Well, I know because the authors feel responsible for it. In all, the article was like a balsam – a more straightforward rendering of the issue is, I believe, impossible.

At the same time it is surprising how little response it generated. I have not come across many statements in a similarly direct tone, almost as if such admissions were considered too condescending or premature. Worse still, Polish public opinion (and the media) is strongly divided on the matter; one side accepting the painful truth and attempting to make up for past wrongs, the other denying facts and rejecting all proof in order to protect its innocent image. The chasm between the two is very deep with apparently no communication.

It is hard to judge the relative force of these two camps. Some foreign observers appear to view those in Poland who undertook

[2] "Nasza wina. Przepraszamy Żydów i prosimy o wybaczenie", *Wprost*, March 25, 2001, pp. 26–33.

the task of redefining the Poles' image as a fringe group, rather like Dietrich Bonhoeffer and Father Lichtenberg in Nazi Germany. In fact the situation is totally different, the best proof of which is the stance of President Kwaśniewski. The Jedwabne debate's deep impact is also visible in many Jewish experiences – including mine. Nonetheless the force with which the affair hit home showed how unprepared Poland's population and elites were for these facts about their country.

Besides which, the Kielce pogrom provided ample material for a similar debate to the one that erupted around Jedwabne. That no such discussion arose is a result of the hampering influence of communism.

5. The communist experience merits deep research

Doubtless the communist years did not inspire serious thought. Most important during that period were caution, keeping a constant eye on censorship and its demands, and staunchness in defending one's positions. This hampered the development of a regular debate on Poland. Nevertheless, communism is all too frequently used as a convenient excuse for everything. Just how often do we tell ourselves: it's not our fault, communism is to blame? In fact, however, communism was created by people, with millions involved one way or another. Besides, not everything connected with our present subject necessarily caused conflict between the communists and their adversaries. Let us take the example of Auschwitz. The communists organised an Auschwitz exhibition which hardly mentioned the camp's Jewish victims (in fact the Jews were mentioned – in an alphabetic "nationality list" of inmates which started with Austria). However, would things have been much different if the then opposition or the Church had been in charge of the display? The controversies which emerged in the 1990s suggest that their stance regarding "ownership rights" to Auschwitz would have been similar. In fact, in this rare case the communists were at one with Polish public opinion.

Communism and its experience still lack a sound analysis. Very many still believe that the Jews were responsible for communism and that this explains Jedwabne. This is hypocrisy; nonetheless the presence of Jews in the communist elites is a fact. And, paradoxically, although most Jewish war survivors left Poland, those that remained frequently occupied high government posts (particularly in Warsaw).

To my mind Jewish involvement with communism is a phenomenon warranting serious study. For some Jews, communism even became a quasi-religion, and because of the communist government the mid-twentieth century could witness members of one of the world's most cruelly persecuted social groups not only as victims, but also as oppressors. This is a cause for self-criticism and shame. It does not, however, follow that *only* the Jews have this moral nut to crack. Still, most Jews are very reluctant to admit that communism also poses a moral challenge for them. The Jewish self-image is very one-sided: Jews were among the victims.

Likewise the Poles (and this is by no means their only similarity to the Jews!). The Poles tend to see themselves solely as victims, with communism perceived as an evil superimposed upon innocent people. The years under communism strengthened such beliefs, but their roots go much further back, to the romantic tradition and Polish messianism.

6. Polish romanticism is still the core of Polish attitudes

In my belief many familiar attitudes (for example, the above-mentioned obsession with innocence, rivalry as to who suffered most, etc.) take their beginnings in concepts like "Poland as the Christ of Nations." Although historically distant and seemingly outdated, such ideas were constantly fanned high by Poland's national poets. And this is why some controversies are so difficult to resolve today: both sides see themselves as "chosen nations". This is also why most Poles today still believe they suffered more, or at least as much, as the Jews during the war years.

The Poles' "chosen" status is a concept familiar only to the Poles, the Jewish nation's mission is known throughout Western civilisation. Some authors nevertheless try to offer a deep and just picture of Polish messianism. A good example here is Maria Janion, whose studies on the subject contain both criticism and fascination. Janion criticises Polish messianism's compensatory function, its tendency to dehumanise aliens, its conviction that "we're not to blame", and its belief that the Poles deserve the world's gratitude. At the same time such a stance can be fascinating: fascinating through its force, scope, religious roots, artistic abundance and consolatory qualities. I doubt that a similarly subtle analysis was ever carried out on Polish messianism's prototype – Jewish messianism (although I must add that I am probably insufficiently abreast of debates on the matter in Israel. Still, even if they are attempted, they have neither influenced Israel's traditional religious circles nor its non-believers, nor average U.S. Jews).

Romanticism brings to mind a more distant period – the First Polish Commonwealth (up to the end of the eighteenth century). It is often said that it was a Jewish haven and, although this should not be taken at face value, it is to an extent true. At the time most Jews actually lived in Poland. They had their place in society, whose integral part they formed, and better development prospects than their compatriots in Western Europe. It is therefore no wonder that reconciliation-seeking Poles (and Jews) today often refer to this phase in Polish history as a basis for a new accord between both peoples and forgiveness of past wrongs. Unfortunately, however, I don't believe this will bring the desired effects.

7. No Polish-Jewish reconcilement is possible through First Commonwealth references

The First Commonwealth is not very deeply embedded in average Jewish awareness and neither are collective memories of a common Polish-Jewish fate. True, there is some sentiment relating to Polish regions, places, names, etc. (interestingly most alive among religious traditionalists), but they do not extend to the First Commonwealth years. Jews (with the exception, of course, of Jews educated in Polish schools) remember bygone days in Poland mostly through the prism of Europe's and Christianity's stance towards them, and, moreover, everything is always viewed from the Holocaust perspective – and not only by Jews.

8. The Holocaust is a factor in Christian-Jewish universal dialogue

The Holocaust is a challenge for European civilisation and Christianity. The fact that the Church's "teachings of contempt" paved the way for Auschwitz is something not only the Germans and their helpers in the Holocaust, but all Christians must come to terms with. In keeping with century-long teachings, the Jews, descendants of Christ's murderers, were contaminated, guilty and contemptible, Luther himself even stating that "their synagogues, houses and books should be burnt".

This European dimension of Jewish history is rarely taken into consideration in Poland. The Germans persecuted us too, the Poles usually say, and this is more relevant than the fact that we share the Church with them. We should rather remember how we suffered with the Jews.

The Poles' sufferings are a fact and in Poland they tend to overshadow the Jewish tragedy. Strangely enough the Holocaust did not change the Poles' stance towards the Jews although it happened right before their eyes. Changes in this respect have generally been imported from the West.

In a way Poland is done an injustice here; the Church's, Europe's and Germany's history which associates with the Holocaust – the most horrendous display of antisemitism ever – is all too easily linked to those who were closest to it, who inhabited the area around Auschwitz: the Poles. On the other hand, what is good – the Church's new teachings and the shock evoked by the Holocaust—is not associated with Poland at all. This results from historical burdens which are especially heavy in Poland's case. Also not to be forgotten are certain facts which distinguish Poland negatively (although this would be easy to change). The best example are pictures in Sandomierz Cathedral which still show ritual killings without a word of commentary. In this situation can one really wonder that Israeli tourists are all too apt to see Poland as the Shoah's breeding-ground?

While we're on the subject, I must stress that Poland's stance towards Israel is no major problem today and although the Poles do not know much about Israel, anti-Israeli attitudes are relatively rare.

9. Property restitution: difficult and unresolved

Millions of people in Poland lost their belongings, millions were forced into resettlement. These matters were a taboo until recently but it must be said that both Jews and non-Jews lost a lot in the process. I believe the issue should be included in a general and possibly just resolution plan, though I do understand that there can be no simple solutions here, as a new status quo has emerged and all restitution means a loss for those who over decades have settled into the property that had belonged to someone else so long ago.

Let us, however, take a look at this through the eyes of former Polish Jews and their descendants. After losing their next of kin, miraculously surviving a true Gehenna and having their property confiscated after the war, they are now told by post-communist Poland that these are past issues that cannot be resolved. Of course, the actual words said – and perhaps even some of the intentions – are different, nevertheless we have not come any closer to a restitution law. Poland refuses to admit the advantages it reaped from the Holocaust, restitution supporters say, forgetting history and its complications, the losses suffered by the Poles and their various post-war tragedies. Is it right to turn a deaf ear on restitution claims? I don't ask whether it is politically correct in light of the influential U.S. Jewish lobby or Poland's limited financial capabilities. Both factors must, of course, be remembered and will result in compromise. However, the fundamental issue here is whether Jewish – and not only Jewish – property claims are justified. Is ignoring them *morally* right? The answer to this question will also determine the political and financial solutions in this matter – solutions reached in the belief that restitution claims are right (even if difficult to fulfil) will differ greatly from those adopted in the conviction that the whole issue was imposed on the Poles from outside.

Can one be a sincere supporter of Polish-Jewish reconciliation, of apologising for bygone sins and of uprooting antisemitism and at the same time oppose Jewish property claims? In other words, can one accept moral claims and simultaneously reject the material ones?

I have no doubt that many really think this way. What, however, does this signify? In what kind of light does it place such people? People who are truly sorry for antisemitism, who are against the teaching of contempt, are ashamed of Jedwabne, respect Jews and feel sincerely sorry for the Holocaust victims – but refuse to back their claims to material compensation. In other words, people who are ready for anything as long as it doesn't cost anything. Does this not undermine their credibility in the non-material sphere?

What are apologies worth without compensation? Is this not a bit too cheap?

It is not for me to answer. I repeat: I do not deny the true difficulties and the purely physical inability to satisfy all. I too would feel relieved if those claiming restitution – Jews and others – decided to resign their claims. Nevertheless, it is one thing to make such decisions of one's own accord and another to expect them from others.

10. Reconcilement with the past is a long and winding road demanding constant repetition of the above truths

At the close of their remarkable article, Janecki and Mac mention Jewish expectations of a plea for forgiveness: "This will not be done by a simple sorry, even uttered by the President. We should all apologise – together and individually".

These are well-chosen words but they embarrass me. Who is to apologise to me? People I know? My family? My friends? There is something not quite right here. Although, as I said above, I myself feel like saying "I forgive" to those who ask for it, I nevertheless know I have no right to apologise on behalf of those who died. Neither do I have the right to receive apologies. What I can – and want to – do, however, is to tell them "Thank you!"

Jews, Communism And The Jewish Communists

Note

This paper studies the problem mentioned in the title, primarily with a Jewish audience in mind. The message is that communism does pose a moral problem to Jews. It was presented in various places, and in essentially the present form at the Central European University in Budapest, in March 1997. The final text was modified in May 1999, and published in a CEU annual *Jewish Studies at the Central European University*, ed. by Andras Kovacs, co-editor Eszter Andor, CEU 2000, 119-133.

Ten Theses

1. Marxism, radical leftist ideologies, and "real socialism" constitute not only a fragment of world history, and of Polish or Hungarian histories, but also a chapter in Jewish history.

2. Antisemites have grossly exaggerated the Jewish involvement in communism, distorted the facts, and interpreted them according to mythical conspiracy theories. Jews were also victims of communism.

3. Jewish communists rarely cared about Jewish concerns and often virtually stopped being Jewish.

4. Some of those who had abandoned Jewishness later came back. The number of Jewish communists, and their role, was so important that other Jews must not ignore it.

5. The deepest problem is posed by the quasi-religious character of the communist involvement of some Jews.

6. There is no distinctive Jewish radicalism. There is no "Jewish Communism". Jews became communists because of general social trends.

7. It was not Judaism or Jewish traditions but the social situation that led Jews to communist involvement.

8. Participation in evil can begin with noble and selfless intentions.

9. Moral responsibility can be indirect. Re-emerging Jewish communities in Eastern Europe should face the legacy of Jewish

participation in communism. However, accepting a Jewish share of moral responsibility does not make non-Jews less responsible.

10. Objective research is needed to clarify the extent and the nature of the Jewish participation in communism. The tragic consequences of the antisemitic myth of "Jewish Communism" should impose no taboo.

Introductory remarks

The phrase "Jews and communism" brings to mind to two sets of immediate associations.

The first image, common in the West, is that of the *persecutions* of Jews in communist countries: the destruction of religious traditions; the doctors' plot, and more generally Stalin's antisemitism that almost led to large scale murder of Jews; the fate of *refuseniks* and discrimination against Jews in the Soviet Union; official antisemitism in Poland in 1967-68.

The second set of associations, popular in East Central Europe and beyond, is expressed as the image of "Jewish Communism": Jews as the founders of the leftist movements and as communist leaders in the states that were governed by communist parties; persecuting Christian religions, pre-eminent in the bloody communist dictatorships.

Now, the first image is true but it does not represent the total picture of the relationship of Jews with communism. The second image is false but it does point to certain facts, specifically to the large number of Jews among active communists. As Andre W.M. Gerrits put it, the power of the association of Jews with communism comes from the fact that "it was based on elements of fiction *and* reality."[1] The myth of "Jewish Communism" is only a myth. What is real is the existence and importance of *Jewish Communists*. The distinction made by Gerrits, had been made earlier by Jaff Schatz in the most important book length study of the topic[2], and also by myself[3]. This reality has been subjected to surprisingly little research.

1 Andre W. M. Gerrits „Antisemitism and Anticommunism. The Myth of „Jewish Communism" in Eastern Europe", *Dialogue and Universalism* 11-12/1995, 27-51, p.32.

2 Jaff Schatz *The Generation. The Rise and fall of the Jewish Communists of Poland*, University of California Press, 1991.

3 In an article "Żydzi a komunizm" ("Jews and Communism", in Polish) published in the

The neglected topic - which I propose to consider now - is then not so much "Jews and communism", or "Jews under communism", and certainly not "Jewish Communism", but rather "Jewish communists". In addition to seeing this topic as a subject for scholarly research I propose its less objective variant: "Jewish communists as a Jewish concern."

My remarks can serve only as an introduction to a problem that in my opinion deserves study by scholars and reflection by Jews, even those who have never met a communist.[4]

It should be also mentioned that my interest is not devoid of personal motivation. In 1970's I read a remarkable book of conversations between two great writers, Czeslaw Milosz and Aleksander Wat, *Pamiętnik mówiony* (Spoken Diary, in Polish). Wat recalled that a certain communist leader functioned as a "Tzaddik" to his followers. That leader, Adolf Warski, one of founders of the Communist Party, later member of Polish parliament, murdered in Russia during Stalinist terror, happened to be my great-grandfather.

underground periodical *Krytyka* 15/1983, 178-206, under my then pen name Abel Kainer. It was published in English in: *From the Polish Underground, Selection from* Krytyka *1978-1993*, ed. by Michael Bernhard and Henryk Szlajfer, Pennsylvania State University Press, 1996, 353-394.

4 Of course the topic has been approached by some scholars like Jacob Talmon or Erich Fromm, and by writers like Bashevis Singer and Israel Singer, or Polish contemporary writers Julian Stryjkowski and Henryk Grynberg. This is, however, not enough. The theses and many of the comments presented below were published, sometimes in an expanded version, in my book *Żydzi, judaizm, Polska* (Jews, Judaism, Poland - in Polish), Warsaw 1997. Additional considerations are contained in the *Krytyka* article (see previous note).

Comments to the theses

1. Marxism, radical leftist ideologies, and "real socialism" constitute not only a fragment of world history, and of Polish or Hungarian histories, but also a chapter in Jewish history.

Communism constitutes a relatively important fragment of recent Polish or Hungarian history, as well as of the Russian or, say, Chinese histories; clearly it will always remain a chapter in European history, and indeed in the history of our civilization. I propose to consider communism as a chapter of Jewish history, too.

Speaking about communism I mean, first, Marxism and a broader field of left wing radicalism, and, second, the "real socialism" in the countries governed by communist parties. It is the second element, the participation in communist rule, and the resulting responsibility for its activities, that makes the issue of the role of Jewish communists in the framework of the Jewish history highly emotional. If the phenomenon of Jewish communists is seen as part of the comprehensive Jewish history, it follows that in our century, in Eastern Europe, Jews were not only among the oppressed, but were also among the oppressors. Because we Jews were the victims of the most horrible persecutions, the very idea that some of us were among the victimizers sounds dramatic and is hard to accept. Yet it is clearly a fact.

Of course, this thesis about Jews being also among the oppressors can be accepted only if we admit that communists did oppress and persecute. I suppose that very few people deny this. It is however true that the early communists, the revolutionaries from the period of illegal activities, were motivated by the rejection of social injustice. They wanted to create a just society and eventually produced a system of organized terror.

Let me mention just some examples – and these are facts, not myths – showing that communism, and more generally left wing radicalism, was relatively widespread among Jews, especially in Eastern Europe.

Most Jews who left closed traditional communities tended to support radical political ideologies. If they did not choose Zionism they supported the revolutionary left and sometimes both at the same time. The secular Yiddish culture was predominantly leftist.

What is even more relevant, Jews were important in communist movements. Jews were very prominent among revolutionary leaders, both before and after the seizure of power. Occasionally, other leaders praised Jews for this; Engels and Lenin for example.

Reproaching Jews for their radicalism has been common among conservatives. To give less well known examples: in the 1920s, some Swedish experts on Russia had no doubt about the role of Jews. Alfred Jensen (neither pro-Jewish, nor antisemitic) wrote in 1921: "approximately 75 percent of the leading Bolsheviks are of Jewish origin".[5] The Russian Tsar Nicholas II said that "nine-tenths of the troublemakers are Jews".[6] I have no idea how close to or far from the truth this is. Antisemitic usage of such statements has made it very difficult to know whether they refer to facts.

Of course, there is a deep difference between those who became revolutionaries in order to fight injustice and those who supported communist oppression, another form of injustice. Yet usually idealist radicals became functionaries of the system when the opportunity came, or supporters of the new rule, if they lived elsewhere. For instance, both Jewish activists in Eastern Europe and in Israeli kibbutzim were eagerly pro-Soviet in the period of terror in the later years of Stalin's life.

In Poland, immediately after World War II, most Jewish organizations were pro-communist; they saw communists as the force that can bring security and stabilization. To be a Jew was sometimes an

5 Kristian Gerner "Degrees of Antisemitism: the Swedish Example", in: *Jews and Christians, Who is Your Neighbour after the Holocaust?* (ed. Michał Bron Jr.), Acta Sueco-Polonica, No 2, Uppsala 1997.

6 Quote after Jaff Schatz „The Riddle of Jewish Radicalism", manuscript, p.1.

advantage for those ready to make careers in the emerging communist system. (Though it could be a burden; I know examples of the returning individual Jews who were offered career opportunities, and examples of those who were denied them - in both cases Jewishness seemed essential.)

I wish to avoid a misunderstanding. I am not saying that Jewishness was ever sufficient for a career. Not Jews, but loyal persons were needed, preferably those with no family ties. Jews were often perfect candidates; isolated, with no families, not connected to pre-war power elites, dreaming about normal lives and protection by state authorities.

Some Jews in post-war Poland tried to punish those guilty of murder of their families. It is mentioned in some literary works by Jewish survivors, like in the remarkable recent book by a Polish Jewish survivor Wilhelm Dichter[7]; his mother in Lvov asked a Soviet Jewish officer to send a Polish neighbour who had reported her family to the Germans to Siberia. The most dramatic example is provided by the story of Solomon Morel, sadistic head of a concentration camp for Germans in Poland, immediately after World War II.[8]

I am aware that antisemites have abused those facts, distorted them and built on their basis a mythical picture of Jewish conspiracy.

2. Antisemites have grossly exaggerated the Jewish involvement in communism, distorted the facts, and interpreted them according to the mythical conspiracy theories. Jews were also victims of communism.

The view that the phenomenon of Jewish communists must be seen as part of the comprehensive history of Jews is not accepted

7 Wilhelm Dichter *Koń Pana Boga* (God's horse, in Polish), Znak, Kraków 1996.

8 The story was described by Jonathan Sacks in *An Eye for an Eye*, Basic Books, New York 1993.

by average Jews and by many authors. They point to the fact that the existence of Jewish communists was a pretext for antisemites, who used it in their conspiracy theories. It is true that the myth of "Jewish Communism" ("*żydokomuna*", or "jewcommies", in Polish) has been one of the most sinister ideas that shaped European politics; it was used to justify aggressive and violent antisemitism, and eventually led to mass murder by Nazi Germany. And it is still used, in Poland and elsewhere, by demagogue politicians.

It is imperative to remember then all the facts that contradict the idea of "Jewish Communism". Let me mention just a few.

Most Jews were never communist or pro-communist and most communists were never Jewish. Various minorities were over-represented among communists. This was, by the way, a paradox because communists believed they represented the working masses, the national majority.

Most Jews did not support communism. Even in post-war Poland when the choice for Jews was limited (this is also true of Hungary) the majority of Jews were not pro-communist and they mostly left Poland.

Jews were also victims of communism. Some facts, like the doctors' plot, are well known. But the anti-Jewish practice of communism was much more fundamental. Despite possibilities of individual careers, all Jews who wanted to continue specifically Jewish activities, whether they were religious, political, or Zionist, were seen as enemies by communists, including the Jewish communists. Traditional Jewish communal life was destroyed by victorious communists.

What is more, communism created its own myth of "Jewish (Anti-)Communism" in the world Trotskyite/Zionist conspiracy. As a matter of fact, the picture of "rootless cosmopolitans" was used by communists and anti-communists alike.

The persecutions of Jews took place not only when large campaigns against "Zionists" were mounted. In the late 1940's in Poland, when the Jewish communists were most influential, many Jews were sent to prisons, for example for "speculation", that is economic activities. And those who really tried to be active as Zionists could become "prisoners of Zion" in all communist countries.

Antisemitism has always existed on the left. Some revolutionaries, not excluding young Marx, were ready to treat capitalism as an essentially Jewish phenomenon. In fact, the spectre of "Jewish Communism" haunted the communist parties from the very beginning. The overrepresentation of Jews caused "an embarrassment and a political liability" to communist parties. This is a largely neglected story.[9] To give a specific example: in 1948, a short time before his (temporary) removal from the chairmanship of the communist party, Władysław Gomulka wrote a letter to Stalin in which he stated that he saw "the necessity to not only stop increasing the percentage of the Jewish element in the state and party apparatus but rather to gradually decrease this percentage."[10]

Sooner or later in most communist parties there were antisemitic purges with the hope of achieving the "national purification" of the party. That could reveal a deeper phenomenon. As Adam Michnik rightly observed, in Poland, the antisemitic and anti-intellectual campaign of 1968 was the culmination of an attempt to legitimize the regime by appropriating for itself the Polish fascist traditions, together with their virulent antisemitism.

3. Jewish communists rarely cared about Jewish concerns and often virtually stopped being Jewish.

The view that the phenomenon of Jewish communists must be seen as part of the comprehensive history of Jews is not accepted

9 Wrote Gerrits, *op. cit.*, p. 42, 43.

10 The letter was discovered in Russia, and presented to the public by Andrzej Paczkowski (*Gazeta Wyborcza* December 18-19 1993, p. 17.)

by average Jews for another important reason. Jewish communists were so unrepresentative, so far away from the mainstream current of Jewish life that – say many Jews – their activities do not deserve to be part of the Jewish history.

Communists of Jewish descent were alienated, tried to be more "more Catholic than the Pope." They were generally "not especially interested in the Jewish issue".[11] For non-communist Jews the government was never free of antisemitism, even in the presence of Jews in power. One emigrant, Bernard Goldstein, complained that Jews who like Minc, Berman, Zambrowski or Borejsza, occupied the top posts in the communist ruling elite, did not bother to help the Jewish community. "They were hired servants of the dictatorship,"[12] he wrote. Among the most significant features of Jewish communists was their desire to leave the Jewish world, often to stop being Jewish, so that at least their children would have no Jewish sentiments, and no Jewish problems. I, as well as many of my friends, know this from our own experience.

What is even more important, communist practice was invariably directed against Jewish traditions and communal life, and it may rightly be called antisemitic. Antisemitic expression was forbidden but Jewish life was restricted as much as other traditions and eventually even more. It is undeniable that Jewish communists acted not as Jews but as communists; they did exactly the same things that did all other communists in similar positions, and specifically Jewish concerns could not influence their decisions. Even traditional Jews could understand that point. Rabbi Joseph B. Soloveitchik wrote: Jewish Bolsheviks "wanted to convince Stalin that they were first and foremost communists rather than Jews."[13]

[11] Gerrits, *op. cit.*, p. 46.

[12] Quote after one of the most important contributions to the study of our topic, the book by Krystyna Kersten *Polacy, Żydzi, komunizm, Anatomia półprawd 1939-1968* (Poles, Jews, Communism, An Anatomy of Half-truths - in Polish), Niezależna Oficyna Wydawnicza, Warszawa 1992, p.81.

[13] *Midstream*, January 1997, p. 40.

The only exceptions were the communists active among Jews. They stressed their Jewishness but fought against Jewish traditions. The rare Jewish communists who in post-war Poland wanted to be active as Jews referred to "the progressive Jewish nation under the auspices of Comrade Stalin".[14] They expressed Stalinist ideas in the Yiddish language. But even they wanted to finish with Jewish distinctiveness in the long run. They seemed to assume that in the future ideal world there would be nothing specifically Jewish. As proof, they raised children unaware of their Jewishness. In post-war Poland they were also "unhappy about the government's policy to allow Jewish emigration in 1949-1950" and tried "to sabotage it by delaying and otherwise obstructing the issuance of documents required for exit applications."[15]

Communism was, among other things, a form of assimilation. To some, this "red assimilation", to use the phrase of Ozjasz Thon, "that repulsive red assimilation – spiritual desolation among the youth",[16] seemed to be the most promising way. It was often efficient – to a point. When they became rejected or just disenchanted they often "regressed" into Jewishness.

4. Some of those who had abandoned Jewishness later came back. The number of Jewish communists, and their role, was so important that other Jews must not ignore it.

For antisemites the number and visibility of Jewish communists means that communism was Jewish and that Jews were ruling. This is nonsense. In fact, it is easy to show that the presence of Jews was politically inessential, be it in Poland or in Hungary or in other countries. I think it evident that even if there had been no Jews in

14 Kersten, *op. cit.*, p. 78.

15 Schatz, *The Generation*, p. 252.

16 In the introduction to the monumental volume *Żydzi w Polsce Odrodzonej* (Jews in Reborn Poland, in Polish), Warsaw 1928.

these countries after the war, the political developments in the post-Yalta world would have been the same.

If so, is the presence of Jews among communists a noteworthy occurrence? And why should we care now? From the perspective of the contemporary Westerner the story of Jewish communists seems rather exotic, an unimportant dead end of Jewish history.

I disagree. True, they were mostly strongly un-Jewish, that is, they tried hard to abandon Jewishness. Some authors maintain that no relationship existed between their origins and their communism.[17] After all, they clearly did not act as Jews; though many of them later, when the communist world rejected them, came back to the Jewish world. Also, they had Jewish family members. One striking example is Jakub Berman, the second most important person in Stalinist Poland, was very far from Jewish concerns; at the same time his brother, Adolf, was a left-wing Zionist and emigrated to Israel.

Also, many Marxist Jews had a strong Jewish identity and were Jewishly active. Bundists and left wing Zionists believed in socialism and in revolution similarly to communists.

Above all, the size of the phenomenon should not be underestimated. Isaac Bashevis Singer recalled how in 1920's Warsaw, in the coffee shops attended by Jewish writers and journalists "everyone" was looking forward to revolutionary changes, and he alone was "living in the past". We are not speaking about a handful of individuals. It was a social phenomenon; radical leftist alternatives were dominant in some Jewish circles.

Also, it is a fact that Jews holding high official positions in post-war Poland, and also in Hungary, Rumania, Czechoslovakia, Lithuania, were, relatively speaking, very numerous. Not as numerous, though, as the antisemitic stereotype, "they were all Jews." In 1945, in the bul-

[17] This point has been argued by, among others, my father (Warski's grandson): "Fakty i mity. O roli Żydów w okresie stalinowskim." in: *Więź* 5 (1997), 109-122. English translation: "Facts and Myths: on the Role of the Jews during the Stalinist Period" in: *Więź Special Issue: Under One Heaven*, Warsaw 1998, 93-110.

letin of the London based Polish Telegraphic Agency, it was stated that "all official positions in ministries and state offices were filled with Jews."[18] Krystyna Kersten reports a private note by Bierut, the leader of Stalinist Poland, who recorded that while there were 438 Jews among 25,600 employees of the state security forces (1.7%) among the top 500 security officers there were 67 Jews[19] or 13.4%. According to internal statistics in the Polish Ministry of Interior, made available by Andrzej Paczkowski, in the period 1944-1956 almost 30% of top officers were Jewish.[20] In 1953, Ostap Dłuski wrote that in the Ministry of Foreign Affairs there were "8 directors of departments of which 5 were Jews, for the 12 available posts of deputy directors only 4 were nominated, among which 3 were Jews, and of 28 division managers 18 were Jews."[21]

In Poland, "Żydzi w UB", that is "Jews in the security forces" has become a standard image. It does express antisemitic attitudes. There is no reason to believe that those posts were occupied by those Jews because they were Jewish. But even rejecting the stereotype and the generalization it is wrong to ignore the above mentioned figures as irrelevant. The "rule of Jews" was perceived – and continues to be seen – also by persons who were far from antisemitism. In 1996, posthumous diaries of two important personalities were published in Poland: the widely respected major writer Maria Dąbrowska, and another well known writer and journalist, Stefan Kisielewski. Anti-communist Kisielewski wrote both that "Jews have always loved communism" and that "Poland without Jews is the saddest possible Poland".[22] Both writers mentioned "the ruling Jews" as an obvious fact of Stalinist Poland.

[18] Kersten, *op.cit.* p. 79

[19] Kersten, *op.cit.* p. 83-84.

[20] "Aparat bezpieczeństwa" in: *Instytucje Państwa Totalitarnego*, research report of the Institute of Political Studies PAN, 1994, p. 61.

[21] Quoted after a manuscript by Dariusz Stola "The Anti-Zionist Campaign in Poland 1967-1968", endnote 10, p. 79.

[22] Stefan Kisielewski *Dzienniki 1968-1980*, Iskry, Warsaw 1996.

Probably part of the impression came from the fact that during World War II Jews were seen as victims, only victims and nothing but victims. And suddenly they were important, the "resurrected Judas."[23] The image of Jews participating in power elite, and as a matter of fact participating in state administration incomparably more than had been the case in pre-war Poland, was so strange to Poles that it was seen as suspicious.[24] Despite all those reservations, the fact remains that communist Jews were numerous and influential. I believe that this fact should be incorporated into the thinking on Jewish history by scholars and by average Jews, though to me the sheer number of communist Jews is not the only and not even the most important aspect of the problem.

5. The deepest problem is posed by the quasi-religious character of the communist involvement of some Jews.

I can certainly understand Jews being pro-communist in certain periods. In the polarized Poland of 1946 they had unfortunately little choice of allies. Communists could be seen as the only force that could efficiently defend Jews against antisemitism. This resulted in a vicious circle: the more Jews were afraid, the more they relied on communist authorities – and at the beginning of the post-war period on the Red Army itself[25] - the more they were threatened, and the more afraid they became. It was hard to step out of the circle. What then is the problem (that I see as a Jewish problem)?

The character of the alliance of Jews with communist rulers was not predetermined. The cooperation of Jewish leaders with victori-

[23] Aleksander Smolar "Tabu i niewinność" (Taboo and Innocence, in Polish), *Aneks* 41/42 (1986), 89-133, p. 110.

[24] This aspect has been stressed by Jan Tomasz Gross in *Upiorna dekada* (The Horrible Decade, in Polish), Universitas, Kraków 1998.

[25] This was described by Henryk Grynberg in the novel *Zwycięstwo* (Victory, in Polish).

ous communists was rather natural.[26] What they could have avoided was the quasi-religious zeal with which so many of them assumed the communist positions. For some this had began much earlier.

Revolution was perceived in quasi-messianic terms by some Jews. The fanaticism of the early revolutionaries was not weaker than in the most extreme religious sects. The party became their family, and Stalin their Messiah. To understand the phenomenon of communism, we must perceive it as a quasi-religious movement. Jewish leftist intellectuals produced commentaries to Marx, treating his work much as "holy" scripture. According to testimonies gathered by Schatz, in pre-war prisons they formed communist "yeshivot", adapting Talmudic dialectic "pilpul" methods to the study of their literature.[27] After World War II the pre-war communists entered the state of "holy madness". Even those who survived in Russia were not shaken in their faith. Messianic anticipation was transformed into enthusiasm. Politics was perceived "in truly mystical terms. (...) They saw themselves as active in (...) a practical beginning of he new era."[28]

Ex-communists often presented their experience using the metaphor of the "God who failed". Sergey Bulgakov described revolutionaries as adherents of "religion founded on atheism".[29] Nicolay Berdyaev was among the first who showed that secularized Messianism is the key to understanding modern revolutionaries; modern – and obviously not only Jewish.

It must be stressed that fanaticism was characteristic of all "believing communists" (as distinct from pragmatic career communists in the period of communist rule) and not just Jews (let me remind the reader of North Korea). Those who were Jewish expressed their quasi-religious zeal in a Jewish style. The messianic-like intensity, and the uncritical belief that communists would finish with antisemitism

[26] Cf. the chapter about the cooperation of Jews with state security in Gross, *op. cit.*
[27] Schatz, *op. cit.* p. 138.
[28] Schatz, *op. cit.* p. 249.
[29] Quote after I. Shafarevich, *Le phénomene socialiste*, Paris 1977, p. 267.

as well as with all discrimination against anyone, made them ready to use any means to make possible the building of the new communist order. That is why even well-meaning and humane people could participate in the system of terror.

I see a deep problem here, and a matter of concern for Jews, because it shows the dead end of the Jewish religious fervour and messianic yearnings when directed to false gods.

One can ask, however: how important is the Jewishness of those leftists and communists? If this is just a matter of style, perhaps it is irrelevant?

6. There is no distinctive Jewish radicalism. There is no "Jewish Communism". Jews became communists because of general social trends.

Is the Jewishness of Jewish communists relevant? My answer is that it may be irrelevant but we have no right to assume it. It needs proof; otherwise we would do in reverse just what antisemites do when they assume that communism has Jewish nature. What must be recognized is the existence of a genuine problem here.

Have some elements of Jewish tradition or Jewish condition influenced the ideology and practice of communism? A full answer can be given only as a result of the pursuit of a comprehensive research program.

Antisemites in Europe have often said that Jews created communism and that communism is Jewish. Already in 1879 a report written by Prussian police contained the conclusion that "Jewry is by nature a revolutionary movement."[30] Also Kisielewski, who never was antisemitic, wrote that Jews "created communism". He added that they "should be punished for this" but the ruling communists "punished them for alleged treason against communism." Is there

[30] Jaff Schatz, "The Riddle of Jewish Radicalism", manuscript, p. 1.

a sense in which communism can be reasonably seen as a Jewish creation? Clearly, Jews as a group did not create communism, even if Jews were prominent among its founders. Also, organized Jewish communities were not lovers of communism, even if some individual Jews were.

A comparison will be instructive. Christianity is really a Jewish creation, or rather it was at the beginning. All its founders were Jewish; it started as a Jewish sect. Communism has never been a Jewish sect in any of its forms. In addition, Christianity depends on its Jewish, or Hebrew, roots, and must always ponder their significance. Nothing like this has ever been the case with Socialism or its many currents. If we look at the sources of communism we see a highly complex picture. We can find its forerunners as far back as the states of ancient Egypt or China, and the political philosophy of Plato. The other sources were listed by Erich Fromm: "Marxist and other forms of socialism are the heirs of prophetic Messianism, Christian Chiliastic sectarianism, thirteenth-century Thomism, Renaissance Utopianism, and eighteenth-century enlightenment."[31] It makes no sense to call communism a Jewish creation even in the sense that applies when Christianity is called Jewish.

Still, it is possible to ask whether there are features of communism that make it "Jewish" in some sense. How deep were the similarities of Judaism with communism, and more generally ideologies based on Marxism? Some authors stress the importance of Jewish cultural heritage, especially Messianism, the prophetic traditions, the stress on social justice, the imperative to mend the world. Melvin Lasky believes that a line can be drawn "from the anger of the Biblical prophets to the modern storminess, associated with 1917."[32]

To understand the phenomenon of communism we must see it as a quasi-religious movement. Abraham Kaplan noticed that the Communist

[31] Fromm, *Marx's Concept of Man*, cited in: Melvin Lasky *Utopia and revolution*, London 1977, p. 66.

[32] Lasky, *op. cit.* p. 67.

Party became "in effect, a priesthood."[33] One can be even more specific. According to Kaplan, "the communist myth of human history begins with the Eden of what they call primitive communism; man is then cursed with class differences and the class struggle, moves through the trials of a feudal and bourgeois period, enters the purgatory of Socialism, and is redeemed at last in the heaven of communism. Production takes the place of Providence, ownership is sin, revolution is redemption."[34] What is apparent in this elegant parallel is not so much similarity with Judaism but rather a structural affinity to Christianity. The result of the analysis is completely different from the intent of those who maintain that the nature of communism is Jewish. There is no objective reason to stress its Jewish elements rather than the Christian ones. This reminds me an elderly Jew from the Warsaw synagogue who said he was communist in the sense Jesus was a communist!

Those who practice the Jewish religious tradition rarely become radicals or revolutionaries. The Jewish ideal of *tsedek* is inconsistent with the revolutionary ethos. The cultural heritage is not sufficient by itself to explain the choices of Jewish communists; while some elements of tradition support leftist and radical approaches, others favour conservatism. The tradition is comprehensive enough. The problem remains why one is selected and not the other.

According to some, there exists a Jewish tendency to extremism, or radical solutions. Perhaps so, but this is not sufficiently specific. Similar characteristics are attributed for instance to Russians (Bierdyaev: "Communism suits the Russian soul.") and to the French (Proudhon: Jacobinism is "a kind of moral pestilence special to the French temperament."[35])

My opinion is that although there are similarities between the Judaic tradition and the communist thinking, they are not deep. The

[33] Abraham Kaplan, *The New World of Philosophy*, Vintage, New York 1961, p. 188.
[34] Kaplan, *op. cit.* p. 173.
[35] Lasky, *op. cit.* p. 78.

connection between Jews and leftist ideas and practice is not of an absolute character but is limited to specific time and place. The communist fanaticism of Jews often contained Jewish ingredients but there has been no specifically Jewish radicalism.

I completely agree with Jaff Schatz's solution to the "riddle of radical Jews"; there is no "Jewish radicalism", there are only radical Jews.[36] Individuals become radical in result of a process, governed by general mechanisms, and functioning in their specific situations. For Jews it was a Jewish situation, and Jewish heritage played a role.

Communism is not a Jewish product. Or rather, it is certainly no more Jewish by origin than many other ideas of Western civilization, including Christianity. At the same time it is true that Jews were prominent among European and American (but not Asian) communists. The correct question is not "Why did they create communism?" or "Why is communism Jewish?" but rather "Why was communism attractive to Jews?"

7. It was not Judaism or Jewish traditions but the social situation that led Jews to communist involvement.

There is no distinctive Jewish radicalism. There existed, however, processes leading Jews to leftist radicalism. They had little to do with Jewish traditions but very much to do with the situation of the Jews. The Biblical tradition of social justice only sometimes led to revolutionary involvement. It all depended on the social situation of Jews.

The mechanisms responsible for communist involvement were universal. For example, feelings of hopelessness always lead to radical attitudes. In the case of Jews, lack of hope for satisfactory careers in a society permeated by antisemitism resulted in the belief in the necessity of a revolutionary change of the social order. Hopelessness was widespread in pre-war Europe and led to political radicalism.

[36] In his the book *The Generation* and the article "The Riddle of Jewish Radicalism."

For Jews only the left wing radicalism was available, as the right wing radicals were deeply antisemitic. Only Zionism provided Jews with a way of being both radical and right wing.

In Poland before World War II there were very limited career prospects for bright Jewish youth. These young men and women were not socially accepted. The reds were an exception. This led to a paradox: while communism was to some Jews, and other minorities, a way to assimilation, they remained mostly among people similar to themselves, thereby perpetuating a minority status.

Speaking about the hopelessness I do not mean poverty. Poor people never supported communism only because of poverty. Many remained conservative. On the other hand, it is extremely significant that some children from wealthy families became Marxists or even professional revolutionaries. They did not have to escape poverty, rather they believed in a mission to help others escape poverty. Jews figured prominently among those idealists.

Another general mechanism was the attraction of radical views for marginalized intellectuals. They were important in cultural life, and in radical politics. According to Isaac Deutscher, the revolutionary "non-Jewish Jews" transcended the particularistic and strove for the universal. Before two world wars alienation of assimilated Jewish intelligentsia was often painful. They were neither part of the traditional Jewish community nor were they accepted in the Gentile society. Marginality led to self-hatred, an internalization of antisemitism. The double marginality, ethnic and religious, produced revolutionaries who "seek to have the non-Jews become like them, alienated from traditional religious and national values. Only then will these revolutionaries cease to feel alienated."[37]

There is a simple proof that it was the situation rather than tradition that led Jews to communism. In contemporary Israel, though

[37] Denis Prager and Joseph Telushkin, *Why the Jews? The Reasons for Antisemitism*, Simon and Schuster, New York 1983, p. 60.

not in the first decades of the state, the communist party has been predominantly Arabic. Again, this was caused by their social situation and not by any fundamentally Islamic or Arabic characteristics of communism.

While the mechanisms that caused Jewish participation in communism were general, the whole phenomenon does constitute part of modern Jewish history. Every radical, revolutionary, or fanatic has his or her own reasons for this attitude. They are partly personal, and can partly reflect one's condition or status resulting from belonging to one group or another. For Jews those reasons reflected the Jewish condition. In this sense they were Jewish.

Those Jews had Jewish reasons, even if shallowly Jewish, and brought a Jewish colour to the leftist revolutionary movements.

8. Participation in evil can begin with noble and selfless intentions.

One could still ask why one should remember the Jewishness of those communists, especially of those who did not want to be part of the Jewish people, as part of Jewish history? My answer is that what Jews did is usually taken as part of Jewish history, even if they did not act as Jews. Lists of outstanding Jewish sportsmen are compiled for Jewish encyclopaedias; why not make one of the top Jewish communists? Jewish communists did not represent Jewish interests (and Jewish Olympic medal winners did not represent Jews) but they were perceived as Jews by others, Jews and non-Jews alike.

Even if the above is accepted one could still say that these facts belong to history and there is no reason to remember them. I disagree. My answer is that, the story first poses a most important *moral problem*. This is my personal motive for the thinking about the subject. I am not a historian. But I am a committed Jew and I have ancestors who were communist leaders.

Leftist radicalism contained an inherent evil. Jewish communists took part in a system of terror. I do not say that they had sinister intentions. The intentions were often pure, and sometimes very noble indeed. I, for one, have ancestors who were communists, and I know that they did not want to do evil. In fact this is precisely the reason why the lesson offered by their story is significant. It can be instructive to all.

Their history can teach us something about the traps that not only Jews can encounter. The danger is universal. We have seen many idealists-turned-terrorists or fighters-with-oppression-turned-oppressors. Any case study can help us understand the mechanism of that change. And the story of Jewish communists provides some excellent material for study.

If communists had not seized power we would have seen them mostly as idealists, fanatics, but essentially harmless. The innocence of the early revolutionaries is best illustrated by a story that happened in Kałuszyn in the Russian part of Poland, in 1905. Three young revolutionaries came to the rabbinical court of the town; one shot a revolver into the cupboard and demanded "the money that the bourgeoisie entrusts when they come to settle disputes." They were shown a little money entrusted by poor orphans, brides and widows as their inheritance or dowries. Wealthy people left promissory notes, which were of no use for the intruders. Then the youth said: "Listen, rebbe, we won't take money from poor orphans and widows, although we're desperately in need of money." They also said that they would send one of their men the next day to fix the hole made by the revolver. Shortly afterward they left, shouting "Long live the revolution!" And then the Rebbe said to his colleagues: "You see? A Jewish soul cannot be fathomed. Even their path includes pity toward widows and orphans, and on account of that God will forgive them."[38]

[38] Sefer Kalushin. Quoted after: Jack Kugelmass and Jonathan Boyarin *From a Ruined Garden*, Schocken, New York 1983, p. 118-119.

This Romantic view of revolutionaries is still shared by some of my American and Western friends who remember the idealistic leftists who cared about justice. Because, however, communists took power, and created a system of terror and oppression, even those communists who themselves did not participate in the power elite – like the Western communists or those who had died before – have been included in the universe of evil perpetrated by those communists.

This is clearly a challenge to all communists, not only to the Jewish ones. To me the drama of the Jewish revolutionaries is closer and more relevant. I can sympathize with their dilemmas. I can understand the feeling that only a radical reconstruction can mend the world that produced Hitler and the Shoah. At the same time I am horrified by the consequences of their choices and I feel ashamed. What is more, I believe that all Jews should understand the drama and share the feeling of uneasiness.

9. Moral responsibility can be indirect. Re-emerging Jewish communities in Eastern Europe should face the legacy of Jewish participation in communism. However, accepting a Jewish share of moral responsibility does not make non-Jews less responsible.

Of course, I am not responsible for the bad things done by Jewish communists, even if some of them happened to be my ancestors. The same is true of an overwhelming majority of Jews. American or Sephardic Jews cannot be held responsible, and most of them have had no personal connection to Jewish communists.

Guilt can only be individual. Yet I can be ashamed. Even those Jews who were actively opposed to communism can feel shame. From the Jewish religious point of view it is not irrelevant what other Jews do, even non-religious and anti-religious ones. The whole house of Israel, including the rebellious members, is the partner of the Covenant. If one sees the Jews according to a Talmudic principle, assuming all of us to be "responsible for one another" (*Kol Israel arevim ze ba ze*), then it is hard to deny that communist ideology and even more the communist practice have created a problem for all Jews.

Moral responsibility can be indirect. It is like a family; if a family member does something wrong I feel bad and the stronger the identification, the stronger the feeling. Even from a completely secular perspective the fact that so many Jews lost their minds in their belief in communism can be disquieting.

Also, there exists a logical argument. If one can feel a pride because of an accomplishment of a Jew, even of a non-Jewish Jew who did not act as a Jew, then by the same token one can feel shame because of crimes committed by Jews. If someone ever felt pride because of Freud's accomplishments he should be ready to feel ashamed because of Kaganovich in Russia, or Berman in Poland. One either has the justification for both feelings or neither.

Jewish communists have left a disturbing legacy that needs to be confronted by the re-emerging Jewish communities in East Central Europe. This is not to say that Jews are guilty and non-Jews are not. That is an antisemitic opinion and I have nothing to do with it. Accepting a Jewish share of moral responsibility does not make non-Jews less responsible or less morally involved. The problem of communist crimes remains a challenge for the political left (obviously, I do not propose to ignore the crimes committed by the political right) and for many groups and nations.

It should be evident that I do not try to free anyone from blame, but I have seen these theses on Jews and communism make people think that I speak about the Jewish moral responsibility in order to absolve Christians, Poles, and everyone else. This is not the case. Communism was the trouble, not the Jews.

Conclusion

10. Objective research is needed to clarify the extent and the nature of the Jewish participation in communism. The tragic consequences of the antisemitic myth of "Jewish Communism" should impose no taboo.

I have argued that the Jewish communists, taken together, formed a category that belongs to the history of Jewish people. (Theses 1 through 4.) Jaff Schatz compares the place of Jewish communists within the general history of Jews with that of the followers of Sabbatai Zvi.[39]; no more but no less.

There is no simple formula that explains the problem of the relations between Jews and communism, or answers the question "How Jewish were Jewish communists?" Also, there is no simple answer to the problem of the affinity between Jewishness and communism. One must apply a variety of explanations; first, by referring to the cultural and religious background in order to explain the Jewish flavour of communist activities. Second, taking into account the social situation of Jews in order to understand how the general psychological mechanism leading to radicalism functioned in the case of Jews. (Theses 5 through 7.)

Only antisemitic myths provide simple solutions; they usually express a vision of a Jewish world conspiracy. According to the notorious book on the "Jewish problem" that had dozens of editions in Nazi Germany, Marxism represented the nature of Jews. The author explicitly referred to the tradition of theological, or rather demonological, antisemitism. He wrote that "The Jew is the devil incarnate".[40] This, incidentally, shows that theology is as important in the analysis of antisemitism as it is in the analysis of the processes leading to communism.

39 Schatz, *op. cit.* p.2.
40 Theodor Fritsch, *Handbuch der Judenfrage*, p.236; quoted after Gerrits *op.cit.* p. 35.

Antisemitic nonsense should not stop research on the relationships between Jews and communism. It is not right to deny the existence of any relationship, even though it is true that Jewish communists did the same as other communists. There are people who denounce as racist any attempt to find out the number of Jews among communists and in communist institutions. They even resent any mention that someone was Jewish (by origin). I believe that they propose a virtual taboo because they have not come to terms either with their own Jewish ancestry or with the collective Jewish moral responsibility for the Jewish involvement in communism. If Jewishness is really irrelevant in that story why should it be ignored? Lev Trotsky used to say: "I am not a Jew, I'm an internationalist," but why should we follow his approach? There was no Jewish communism but there were Jewish communists. Discussing them and their role does not have to lead to blaming Jews for all communist crimes.

I have presented above (in Theses 8 and 9) the moral problem posed by the extent and the nature of Jewish participation in the communist enterprise. That activity was not in the name of the Jews, but they were Jews nevertheless. A disturbing legacy has been left for all Jews and in particular for the Jews of East Central Europe and their re-emerging Jewish communities. Talking about that must not be left to antisemites.

Sensitivity and good will is needed to understand the story of Jewish communists. It is a closed chapter so it can be fully described. And this can be instructive all. As the famous anonymous saying goes: "Jews are just like anybody else, only more so..."

An Insert From Another Era:

Solidarity And Martial Law: The Jewish Dimension

Note

The paper was originally written in the mid-1980's and published under the penname Abel Kainer in *Studium Papers* (a quarterly published by The North American Study Center for Polish Affairs, Ann Arbor, Michigan), vol. XIII, No 2, April 1989, pp. 54-59. It is a detailed study of the Jewish-related facts during the initial Solidarity organization of 1980-1981 and under the martial law of 1982-83. I have left it in the original form, only correcting misprints, and adding section titles for better readability, as well as footnotes (incorporating a few footnotes of the original editor). Contrary to the other chapters of this book, this one is more geared to a reader deeply interested in the Polish situation of that time, but at the same time I feel that it conveys something interesting for the general reader, namely the atmosphere and the attitudes of various individuals to things Jewish. Today, I do not necessarily agree with various naïve hopes and sometimes unconscious assumptions, but I retain a deep sentiment regarding those years. I hope the text helps the reader understand why.

For those who are interested, all the important facts relating to the "Jewish question" in contemporary Poland are available and printed in the newspapers. The problem is how to interpret these facts. Since there have been no opinion polls on the subject, one never knows how typical a particular attitude towards Jews is. Any conclusions are bound to be highly subjective. Nevertheless, I will attempt here to examine current Polish attitudes, both official and unofficial, towards Jews. I hope that such an analysis, expressing the viewpoint of someone who spent the first half of the 1980s in Poland,[1] will shed some light on the issue.

Since personal bias is unavoidable in such matters, I will state mine. As a member of Solidarity and an opponent of the present regime, I feel myself both Polish and Jewish. My Jewish identification, although active, remains outside official Jewish organizations, which are completely dependent upon the authorities – as are almost all legal institutions in Poland except for the Catholic Church and some allied organizations. I regret the present state of Jewish-Polish relations; aware of the resentments on both sides. I would like to strive for and see more mutual understanding. What we need most is truth.

It is important to know the true extent of antisemitism in Poland. It has been much deeper and more harmful to Jews than many Poles are ready to admit. Yet it has never been so universal as to support the stereotype, widespread among Jews, that Poles are incurable antisemites.

1. A Weakening of the Taboos

The emergence of Solidarity in 1980 led to a general weakening of the taboos which had reigned supreme in the mass media. The

[1] I always lived in Poland, but I had to hide my identity from the police, so I said something that was untrue suggesting that "Abel Kainer" had lived in the West.

Jewish question was one of hundreds of historical and current problems that could once again be raised and discussed.

Statements condemning antisemitism were not infrequent in Solidarity bulletins. Usually they were specifically aimed at the activities of groups such as the Grunwald Patriotic Union[2], which parroted the propaganda of 1968 that a "Zionist clique" was responsible for the terror of the Stalinist period and anticommunist trends in Solidarity. Wiktor Kulerski, a Warsaw Solidarity leader, denounced Grunwald statements pinning responsibility for Stalinist crimes on "Zionists" as a distortion. Kulerski attacked the Grunwald position for singling out only the Jews from among the oppressors. accusing them of ignoring the role of Soviet superiors, as well as persecutions which continued after the "Zionist" clique was removed. His response was given full support by the Warsaw Solidarity Council.

Solidarity exhibited a similar attitude in Kielce, where union leaders organized a mass in the city cathedral to commemorate the victims of the July 4, 1946 pogrom. The local Solidarity bulletin published an artic1e stating that antisemitism was harmful to Poland and that the instigators of the pogrom had still not been identified. It was Solidarity which broke the silence which had prevailed in public life about this shameful incident.

Among the first discussions of the Kielce pogrom was in the underground monthly *Biuletyn Dolnośląski* (Lower Silesian Bulletin, No. 11, 1980), edited by Jan Waszkiewicz (later elected to Solidarity's National Council). The most extensive account of the circumstances surrounding the pogrom appeared in the penultimate issue of the union weekly *Tygodnik Solidarność* (Dec. 4, 1981). In most peoples' minds the Kielce pogrom came to symbolize the physical danger

[2] Grunwald Patriotic Union; an association of hard-line antisemitic communist Party members. Grunwald, the name of the place where Poles defeated Teutonic Knights (now, for a long time identified with Germans) in 1410, is a symbol generally respected in Poland.

which threatened Jews in postwar Poland. I find this inappropriate, since the event had some unique features. Its length, origin, character, and the use made of it by official propaganda suggest that it was provoked by the authorities. However, it has been admitted by all honest Polish observers that it is only possible to provoke a crowd that is ready to be provoked. The atmosphere was sinister; the Jews were threatened by partisans of the extreme right and by others, especially those who had taken over Jewish possessions. Precious little of this has been mentioned in recent Polish publications. Would the painful facts have been more fully presented if the interlude of freedom under Solidarity had lasted a bit longer? Nobody knows, but I believe they would have; truth, so utterly suppressed by the regime, was a prime concern of Solidarity.

Solidarity was pre-eminently a national movement, reclaiming national values and exploring prospects for greater national independence. Yet simultaneously, Poles discovered the values of pluralism and openness. The revolt against communist uniformity clashed with traditional nationalistic attitudes, xenophobia and antisemitism, and the latter doubtless remained widespread among the millions of Solidarity members. But these nationalistic attitudes did not surface in the movement's policy.

The worker base was central to Solidarity, but it was more than a class movement. All strata were equally represented. The origins of Solidarity stretched back to 1976 and the cooperation between opposition intellectuals and worker activists. Anti-intellectualism, especially in Solidarity's early period, was thus notably absent. Traditionally associated with antisemitism, anti-intellectualism could not disappear totally from private feelings, but experience bad shown that the political and moral strength of the movement depended on everyone working together.

The religious side of Solidarity was also very important. Today the hierarchy of the Catholic Church no longer promotes antisemitism. The Second Vatican Council denounced antisemitism as un-Christian and abandoned theological anti-Judaism. The Council and the attitudes of the post-Vatican II popes strengthened the position of those advocating open Catholicism – in particular, the Catholic intellectual circles which played an essential role in the creation of Solidarity. These groups actively opposed antisemitism.

Nonetheless, traditional teachings about Jews who crucified the Saviour and myths of Jewish-Masonic anti-Christian conspiracies are not easily forgotten, either by the clergy or by the masses of churchgoers. Popular antisemitism has remained widespread, although it is less frequent and more superficial among the younger generations. Older people remember real Jews, once so numerous in Poland, as well as the genuine conflicts their presence engendered; the young tend to repeat stereotypical opinions or attempt to generalize from rare, mostly assimilated Jews in Poland.

Poles are no more and no less willing than other people to listen to bitter truths about themselves. Still, Solidarity encouraged people to be more open and tolerant. In contrast, martial law made it necessary once more to develop a psychological protective shell. In order to facilitate resistance and survival, the need for an optimistic self-image intensified.

2. Themes of the 1968 Antisemitic Campaign

It is important to bear in mind the distinction between antisemitic sentiments and the cold-blooded use of antisemitism in public life. Antisemitism was not one of Solidarity's tools – it belonged to the other side. This does not mean, of course, that all supporters of the government were antisemitic or that the antisemitic feelings of some Solidarity members could not be compared to those of their opponents. All the same, some of the most active groups of hardliners, such as the Party Forum in Katowice or the Grunwald Patriotic Union, were not only antisemitic but made antisemitism an integral part of their ideology. At times this could degenerate into complete pathology. Zdzislaw Ciesiolkiewicz, former head of Grunwald, gave an interview to a Swedish newspaper where he blamed Poland's economic problems on the Jews in Polish institutions, who borrowed excessively from western Jews in an effort to provoke Poland's financial ruin.

Grunwald's revelations ran along the familiar lines of the 1968 antisemitic propaganda campaign. Persons of Jewish ancestry could not be trusted; they contaminate every group to which they belong. Such propaganda was not very successful because antisemitism from above was treated with mistrust. Still, the campaign had a certain logic to it, since it played not only on traditional antisemitism but also used recent facts to buttress its case.

A few of these facts bear mention: Jews were numerous in the communist movement; on average, they were less hostile than Poles to the Soviet invasion of Poland in 1939; most Jews who remained in Poland after the war supported the new regime (of course, the great majority of non-supporters emigrated from Poland); many Jews occupied leading positions in the party and in the police; the policy of Russification and official atheism were not resisted by the Jews to a degree comparable to Poles (after all, the Jews who could have resisted had emigrated); finally, the official policy in the late forties was to honour the1943 Warsaw Ghetto Uprising and at the same time slander the larger Warsaw Uprising of 1944.

In 1981, Grunwald and similar forces sought to recycle these arguments. But this time the propaganda fell on deaf ears. First, this was because there were far fewer Jews remaining in Poland. Furthermore, the campaign in 1968 was considered by many Poles as an essentially internal party affair. Many of the victims of the campaign, the Marxist revisionists and the Jews (some of them only Jews "by nomination"), were not popular. Many were not innocent.

They bad taken part in or had supported similar campaigns of hatred directed against others, notably against the AK (Home Army)[3] and the Church.

Thirteen years later the situation was different. Antisemitism was directed against the democratic opposition and Solidarity, and nobody could consider this as an internal affair of the authorities. In 1968, nobody was able to counteract the antisemitic campaign. In 1981, people spoke out; Grunwald was sharply criticized and often unreservedly ridiculed.

3. Nominal and Real Jews

Antisemitic views appeared in Solidarity during the second half of 1981, but always remained marginal. They were used in internal power struggles. particularly in Warsaw, by persons who were generally called "true" or "genuine" Poles. Antisemitic allusions were directed against the members and associates of the major opposition group, KOR[4], which included several intellectuals of Jewish origin. The attacks against KOR meshed with those broadcast by party bulletins and poster's denouncing some leaders of Solidarity, especially Karol Modzelewski and Bronisław Geremek, for their alleged Jewishness or Zionist-Stalinist-Trotskyite past.[5]

The single most important antisemitic incident within Solidarity was a statement made in November, 1981 by Marian Jurczyk, head of the important union chapter in Szczecin.[6] In a violently anti-

[3] See footnote 15 in Chapter 2.

[4] Workers' Defense Committee, founded in 1976; see footnote 30, Chapter 2.

[5] Both are historians, both are of Jewish origin (though never were in touch with Jewish institutions), and in the past were leftists. Both have been active in the opposition. Modzelewski was a leader of the dissidents in the 1960's and later, and an important figure in Solidarity. Initially active in free Poland he later resigned. Geremek has been an important politician after 1989; he served as the Minister of Foreign Affairs, and was elected to the European Parliament in 2004.

[6] A far right-wing politician in free Poland, he has been elected the mayor of Szczecin.

communist speech he said, among other things, that it was necessary to get rid of all Jews in the government. This comment was made thirteen years after purges which removed all officials of Jewish background from high government positions.

The affair embarrassed other Solidarity leaders and immediately generated statements condemning antisemitism. The responses were not very strong, however, partly because confrontation with the authorities had reached the boiling point, and partly because the introduction of martial law a month after the incident made further responses impossible. In Kulerski's letter mentioned above and in numerous other places it was often repeated that antisemitism was directed principally against Solidarity rather than against Jews. Similar observations have been made when antisemitism was used against the democratic opposition in order to divide and discredit it. This does not mean that this antisemitism was somehow not "real." To question the role of the assimilated Jew is a classic antisemitic motif. What else is antisemitism but reproaching Jews for being Jewish? To reproach somebody for his origins is to put him or her in a hopeless position.

The mere possibility that someone might be Jewish embarrassed those concerned as well as their friends, and often led to a virtual taboo against bringing up a person's Jewish background. Often well-meaning people did not use the word "Jew" in polite company. Although this by itself cannot be regarded as antisemitism, it certainly reflects a society long poisoned by antisemitism. Under these circumstances, one is pushed into Jewishness not only by what others say, but also by their silence – and one's own. This form of "Jewishness" remains purely negative. Although it would satisfy Sartre, it is not acceptable from any Jewish point of view. The problem is relevant here, because the "Jewish question" in Solidarity concerned mostly such extremely "non-Jewish Jews."

Were there any "real" Jews in Solidarity? Could a Jew affirming his identity be accepted as a leader in Solidarity? He certainly could at the grassroots, where everyone knew one another and what mattered most were personal qualities. The higher the level, the more important were general opinions and preconceptions.

One important exception can be said to prove the rule. Marek Edelman, formerly a member of the Bund and a fighter in the Warsaw Ghetto, was an important personality in the democratic opposition in Łódź and later in Solidarity. He was elected a delegate from the Łódź region to the National Solidarity Congress. But neither Edelman, nor any other Jew, participated in Solidarity mainly as a Jew. Rather, they participated as Poles, or simply as citizens of Poland who wanted to take part in the nationwide anti-totalitarian renaissance.

This was also the renaissance of Catholic affirmation. Today's Catholicism no longer teaches antisemitism. The Catholic doctrine of openness excludes no one. Yet a problem remained. Many of Solidarity's Catholic ceremonies could alienate those who were involved in a secular way or were non-Catholics. To be in Solidarity meant to participate in meetings under a cross. True, the cross was widely interpreted as a universal symbol, and the author of this article, for example, did not feel excluded. But this does not mean there was no problem.

There are two Jewish organizations in Poland. One of them is the TSKŻ (Jewish Socio-Cultural Society), with its associated institution, the State Jewish Theatre. The TSKŻ is led by communists for whom the faithful representation of the present party line is no less important than the problems of Jews.

The liberalization of 1980-81 exerted a positive influence upon this organization, as on many others. This could be seen in the widening scope of coverage by its Yiddish-Polish journal *Folks-Shtimme.* Although interesting material would sometimes appear in the journal's pages prior to 1980, political taboos reigned supreme. In 1980, the editors became slightly more militant. They criticized

Grunwald, and denounced the antisemitic campaign of 1968 as being "a deviation from Leninist principles."

The second Jewish organization, the Jewish Religious Congregation, is no less dependent on the authorities. It is smaller and the average age of its members is even higher than that of TSKŻ members. Although some TSKŻ members were in Solidarity, most Jews in both organizations kept their distance. This is not surprising. An analogous situation existed within the Russian Orthodox minorities, Byelorussians, and Ukrainians. On the whole, they also did not join Solidarity. It was not considered to be their organization, despite welcoming gestures by Solidarity's leadership and its journalists.

Beyond Catholicism and the impending confrontation with the authorities, a sociological factor sheds light on the Jewish reticence. The "Jewish Jews" in Poland are old. Solidarity was essentially a movement of the young and middle-aged. Many older people in Poland were against it, longing for peace, law and order at any cost.

4. Foreign Jews Visit

In the Solidarity period, contacts with Israel intensified considerably. Cultural exchange grew as, for example, historians from Yad Vashem came to work in Polish archives.

Official contacts with representatives of foreign Jewish bodies were established. There was a resumption of talks with the Joint Distribution Committee and other philanthropic organizations to resume aid to Jewish institutions in Poland. Other talks resulted in attempts to safeguard neglected Jewish cemeteries. In addition to and independent of this, a Citizens' Committee for the Protection of Jewish Cemeteries and Historical Monuments was established with the aim of raising funds and encouraging local people to take care of ownerless cemeteries.

It is ironic that many of the initiatives begun in 1981 were realized only under martial law. That they were not abandoned is a credit to the junta. Thus, an agreement with the Joint was signed (on December 14, the day after martial law was imposed), several exhibitions took place in Poland, and many books on Jewish subjects which had been prepared for publication in 1981 appeared in 1982-83; more, in fact, than in the previous fifteen years combined.

After an initial freeze, official contacts were resumed with the visit of a delegation of the Joint, headed by its president Henry Taub, and with the arrival of Stefan Grajek, the chairman of the World Federation of Jewish Fighters and Partisans. Representing important Jewish circles, he exerted successful pressure on the government to release Władysław Bartoszewski (who had been active in hiding Jews during World War II and later became a historian of the period, on friendly terms with Jewish historians and survivors). Together with others, Bartoszewski was released in the first week of May 1982.

Jewish official visits from abroad became more numerous than ever before. From time to time, a delegation from Yad Vashem came to award Poles who saved Jews during the war with the title of "Righteous Amongst the Nations", groups of Hasidim came to visit the graves of their rebbes, and so on. The biggest and most heterogeneous group came from Israel and the U.S. in April, 1983 for the commemoration of the Warsaw Ghetto Uprising.

There were discordant notes from officialdom, too. The introduction of martial law in Poland was followed by a series of antisemitic radio broadcasts by the PRL[7] Radio. It was feared that the ideology of the Grunwald Patriotic Union would dominate official policy. Prior to this, the hard-liners had not been taken seriously. They were a minority, but had wide influence in the party, police, and army. Now they gained the upper hand. The propaganda against Solidarity

[7] Acronym for *Polska Rzeczpospolita Ludowa*, the Polish People's Republic, the official name of communist Poland, which evoked negative feelings, and also contempt, among all of us who participated in the anti-communist opposition.

in the army had long been known to contain antisemitic elements. Individuals interrogated by the police were lectured on how Jews manipulated them for their own ends. In one case, the guards transporting a group of women to an internment centre in northern Poland were told (falsely) that the women were all "either unmarried or Jewesses."[8] Presumably, this meant that they were not to be pitied because either they left no children behind or they left only "kikes".

The official antisemitic propaganda in the mass media, however, was muted very quickly for political reasons. Maintaining contacts with Jewish organizations could mean weakening the boycott by the West. In fact, it appears the first Western politicians of some stature to meet high representatives of the military government were Jewish leaders. A1so, the PRL government needed money. Possibly, some PRL leaders imagined that if the Jews were satisfied, they would make loans and credit available, no matter what the political and economic situation.

All these elements – the need for recognition, credibility, and money – formed the background to the *tour de force* of the junta's pro-Jewish policy: the commemoration of the fortieth anniversary of the Warsaw Ghetto Uprising.

The ceremonies were characterized by lavishness and pomp. Poland's borders were opened for all interested Jews, including those from Israel. There were ceremonies in Warsaw as well as other cities and death camp sites. Warsaw's synagogue was rededicated. Everything was extensively reported in the press and on television; everything that was organized by the authorities, that is. Nothing was said about other commemorations or about the controversy among Jews as to whether to boycott the official ceremonies or not.

The main argument in favour of the boycott was that the regime was using the event to legitimize itself. After all, the same regime had commemorated past anniversaries at best in a very modest way.

[8] I know this from my sister who was in that group.

No matter how insincere the authorities were, replied others, this is an occasion to honour the memory of the victims where they had lived and perished. For many this possibility transcended any political considerations. Moreover, it was a unique chance for Israeli citizens to visit the scenes of their youth and to show them to their children.

There were two possible levels of boycott. The first was not to come to Poland at all. Marek Edelman, in his open letter widely publicized abroad, stated that in the Ghetto they had fought in the name of human dignity and since the imposition of martial law was a blow against human dignity, to celebrate in Jaruzelski's Poland would mean to "betray the spirit of our struggle." Similar warnings appeared also in the statement of the Jewish Labour Committee and the Anti-Defamation League of B'nai B'rith. As a result of this argument a number of Jews cancelled their trips. Some Jewish organizations did not send anybody, others (for example, the American Jewish Committee) scaled down their delegations. Although representatives of the World Jewish Congress did come, its president, Edgar Bronfman, did not "in an attempt to prevent the Polish government from politicizing the event." It is estimated that a thousand visitors came, several times fewer than the organizers had expected.

For those who did come and for Jews in Poland a second level of boycott was possible – ignoring the official ceremonies. This could mean either private celebrations alone or participation only in independent ceremonies. One could also choose to attend both the unofficial as well as the official commemorations.

5. Independent Commemorations

While Edelman wrote that "the true memory of the victims and heroes ... will be preserved in the silence of graves and of hearts," a statement signed by "a group of Polish Jews"[9] suggested that the authorities should not be allowed "to take over all the celebrations." They suggested placing flowers "not within the framework of the official celebrations but in peace and dignity at any other time." *Yom ha-Shoah* was suggested as a possible time – it fell on Sunday, April 10, nine days before the Ghetto Uprising anniversary. It was probably by coincidence that a special mass was celebrated on April 10 in St. Augustine's Church, located within the former Ghetto area. The homily by Cardinal Glemp was devoted to the martyrdom of the Jews. The anniversary commemorations were thus begun by the Church.

A further independent initiative was taken up by a specially formed underground committee linked to Solidarity's underground leaders. This committee organized the ceremonies that were to become famous. Although the leaflet they produced was lost in a police search, the information spread out and on April 17 more than a thousand people gathered on the site of the Umschlagplatz, from where 400,000 Jews had been taken to their death in 1942 and 1943.

To evaluate this gathering one has to remember how dangerous demonstrations in Poland were at that time. It was the first demonstration since November 1982, when Solidarity was officially banned. At this ceremony thousands of policemen prevented those present from laying flowers; but it was still possible to lay flowers at the Warsaw Ghetto Monument, despite the presence of innumerable police cars. Edelman, who agreed to participate, was prevented from coming and placed under house arrest in Łódź. He was able,

[9] That small group was composed of several friends of mine (including me).

however, to send a letter, read by Roman Zimand[10], in which he stressed the eternal validity of the values he and other Jews had been defending in their struggle 40 years earlier.

This theme was taken up by Janusz Onyszkiewicz[11], Solidarity' s national spokesperson, who addressed the crowd in the name of the then-outlawed union. Arrested immediately after his appearance, he spent the next three months in jail. In an atmosphere of solemnity and fear of the surrounding police, the participants led by Catholic priests sang patriotic Polish and Catholic songs. It may seem strange, but the author of this article – himself present at this gathering – did not feel that these songs were meant to make the victims "posthumously Catholic." Rather, they were meant to honour the dead and to proclaim values which threatened any totalitarian regime. It was sad that nobody could or dared intone Jewish songs or prayers. Only assimilated Jews were present.

On the next day another independent ceremony took place. Several members of the Home Army (AK) decided to place wreaths on the symbolic graves of the Jewish fighters. They gathered with a few dozen friends at the entrance to the Jewish cemetery, where the group learned that despite earlier arrangements to leave the gate open, the leaders of the Jewish community had ordered the cemetery to be closed. This incident, although not unexpected in view of the total dependence of the Jewish community leaders on the authorities, was nonetheless shameful. Józef Rybicki, commander of a special detachment of the AK which cooperated with Jewish fighters during the war[12], delivered a speech, and wreaths were laid at the cemetery's gate. The wreaths disappeared fifteen minutes later.

[10] Literary critic, formerly a communist, then in the opposition, died in the early 1990s.

[11] Mathematician by training, also an alpinist and politician. In free Poland served as the Minister of Defense, elected to the European Parliament in 2004.

[12] In addition to being an underground AK leader, and a friend to Jews, he was an active senior KOR member.

Many foreign journalists and TV teams came to both independent ceremonies. The chief disappointment for the organizers and for people like the author of this article was the near total absence of Jews from abroad. Their intention, supposedly, was not to play politics. They wished only to honour the memory of the victims and of the heroes, no matter with whom, but in the framework provided by their host, the PRL government.

No matter with whom? They were hoist by their own petard. The PRL organizers invited a PLO delegation and with this ingenious trick created the political balance they wanted. Laying the wreath, the PLO representative made a comment about Israelis as the new Nazis; in a weaker form, this argument appeared on television and in some newspapers (needless to say, all newspapers presented only the official policy). The indignation of the Jews was great, but their protests were infinitely less eloquent than the approval they gave to the government by their very presence at the ceremonies.

The underground Solidarity press marked the anniversary by publishing an interview with Edelman *(Tygodnik Mazowsze*, April 7, 1983) and coverage of the independent ceremonies. Among the latter was a special mass al St. Stanisław Kostka Church, famous for its pro-Solidarity activities. The mass was followed with the recitation of poetry by well known actors and with a speech by Jan Józef Lipski, one of the leaders of the intellectual opposition and a co-founder of KOR.[13] His speech was remarkable because it did not avoid any of the touchy problems of Polish-Jewish relations. He discussed antisemitism, both before and after the War, and the indifference of many Poles to the fate of the Jews during the Holocaust. But he also stressed how unfounded many anti-Polish generalizations are. (His own family was actively engaged in helping Jews throughout the

[13] Literary critic and dissident; in free Poland a Socialist politician till his premature death when we learned with surprise that he was a leader of the Freemasons.

War.) Lipski stressed that although the Polish Jews were murdered, their culture can still enrich Polish culture.

In some underground publications bitterness and even some disgust were expressed because of the presence of the Jewish guests from abroad and, more particularly their one-sided involvement in the official ceremonies. Such responses reflect a lack of understanding by the Polish public. Many Jews and Jewish organizations abroad are not all interested in the political problems in Poland. Relations with Poland interest them only in so far as getting a visa to visit Jewish graves is concerned. At the same time, the extent of the boycott was not sufficiently felt in Poland because of the total censorship and "propaganda success" hailed in the PRL media.

The charge is often made that mounting "competing" ceremonies was unseemly, that it looked too much like a scramble for the memory of the victims. The game, however, was rigged by the authorities, and only two options were left for the opposition. Either do nothing, which would be contrary to the feelings of many opposition-minded people and would allow the regime to monopolize the anniversary, or to organize something, thereby risking unpleasant "competition."

Onyszkiewicz began his April 17 speech by saying that "we did not gather here against anybody." It is a fact, however, that later he stated his belief that the heroes of the Ghetto, if alive, "would join us in our struggle for freedom and dignity." Other underground Solidarity leaders stressed the common ideals of the Ghetto fighters and Solidarity. This feeling is understandable, but no sensible comparison can be made. The Holocaust was unique, not only from the Jewish point of view. Nevertheless, the statements of the opposition paled in comparison to the use made of the anniversary by official propaganda. Whatever one's attitude, what was really at stake was who to consider the real hosts of the Jewish visitors – the authorities or the nation? It can be argued that the authorities do not represent the nation and leaders of Solidarity do. The author understands that this question of who represents Poland is of no concern to those Jews who do not care about Polish-Jewish relations. But for those who do, the unofficial celebrations should be seen as being of the utmost importance, because "Poland was there." (One of the slogans of the anti-regime manifestations is "Poland is here.") With the part of the nation that was represented there, a genuine dialogue can be attempted.

The author wonders if any Jewish organizations pressured the regime to release Onyszkiewicz. His speech was the first public address in the name of Solidarity since the imposition of martial law, and was made a few months after his release from internment. To understand why this fact had a special importance for Jews in Poland, one has to be aware of the atmosphere created by government propaganda in the weeks preceding the anniversary. Television and other media were full of programs and articles about Polish Jews, the war, the Jewish uprising, and above all, about how good the Poles and in particular the present authorities were to the Jews. The manipulative coverage was too much for many people. The authors of the aforementioned letter signed by "a group of Polish Jews" thought it fit to stress that Jews in general do not support the junta and the leaders of the TSKŻ, particularly Szymon Szurmiej, the director of the Jewish Theatre. The letter stated that these Jewish leaders "are no more representative of the Jewish community in Poland than Mr. Dobraczyński (a Catholic writer who is leader of PRON, an officially sanctioned pro-government organization) or Mr. Rakowski represent Polish society." Under these circumstances, the involvement of the opposition and the underground in the independent celebrations had a definite healing quality.

6. Accomplishments

However strange it may seem, despite the scarcity of Jews in the country, the "Jewish question" often provokes passions in contemporary Polish life. Keeping in mind that it is of course a secondary issue, we can identify two conflicting phenomena. On the one hand, there is an increased interest in everything Jewish, on the other, an increase in antisemitism.

For years, Jewish topics – like many topics of Polish history – have been distorted or ignored. School curricula contain very little information about the Jewish presence in Polish history, and many tourist guidebooks do not mention Jews at all in their notes. The Jewish pavilion at Auschwitz was only opened in 1978. This is not to say that there weren't any histories or guide books which treated the subject fairly. There were exceptions, but hardly enough to counteract public ignorance.

There has been improvement since the founding of Solidarity. And as already mentioned, martial law did not alter this trend. Several interesting books have been published including Ringelblum's Warsaw Ghetto Chronicle, Adam Czerniakow's *Diary*, an essay by Zimand on Czerniaków, several novels by Isaac Bashevis Singer, Monika Krajewska's album of Jewish cemetery photographs[14], and an anthology of Polish translations of Yiddish poetry edited by Solomon Łastik and Arnold Słucki (prepared before 1968 and "shelved" for fifteen years by the censor).

In fact, by the late seventies, Jewish subjects and Polish-Jewish relations were already being raised in the underground press. Special mention is due to the activities of the Warsaw Club of Catholic Intellectuals, which for ten years organized "Jewish Weeks" devoted to the symbolic upkeep of Jewish cemeteries, in conjunction with lectures on Jewish subjects. This same milieu of Catholic intellectu-

[14] I would have mentioned the book even if the author hadn't been my wife!

als also produced special issues of the monthly journals *Znak* and *Więź* in 1983, devoted to Jewish history, Judaism, and Polish-Jewish relations. The *Znak* special issue went through an unprecedented second printing of 20,000 copies! Still, the information void was also exploited by antisemites like Grunwald. A book written by J. Orlicki was published in 1984, full of errors and written from a strongly "anti-Zionist" perspective (according to which the Kielce pogrom was organized by Zionists to increase immigration to Israel). Nevertheless, many people welcomed "building bridges between the new generation of Poles and the lost world of Polish Jews and contemporary Jewish thought" *(Znak*, Feb/March, 1983).

How many Poles look at Jews with both interest and sympathy? It is difficult to say. I can say without hesitation that we are also witnessing a strong strain of philosemitism in Poland today. Its manifestations run quite deep. For example, Father Józef Tischner, a leading Polish philosopher who has also served as Solidarity's "unofficial" chaplain[15], taught a course last year on the thought of Franz Rosenzweig and Emanuel Lévinas at the Papal Theological Academy in Kraków.

At the same time, however, an opposite phenomenon can be noticed. What seems to be on the rise now is a developed antisemitism conceived as an ideology explaining world history and Polish problems. As usual, the main charge is that there are too many Jews everywhere (including present-day Poland).

Antisemitic groups have reissued *The Protocols of the Elders of Zion* and other pre-war books by notorious antisemites, occasionally using certain churches as the base of their activities. What is most dangerous is that they consciously appeal to high school-aged youth. In the ideological void now prevailing in public life, young people look for alternatives, and it is often chance that determines whether

[15] Tischner, who died recently, was an important philosopher and a penetrating critic of the Polish condition, which made him, in 1990s, more and more marginalized in the Church, though popular among intellectuals. For a little more on his role, see Chapter 8.

a child encounters a clandestine study group led by open-minded people or antisemites preaching a Jewish-Masonic conspiracy.

These antisemites differ from Grunwald, which is pro-communist, and from antisemites of the Jurczyk variety, who would never suggest that Solidarity was manipulated by the Jews. In their brochures, the new antisemitic groups "expose" the Jewish influence behind not only the party and Solidarity, but even the Church and the Vatican itself.

Active and passive forms of antisemitism have some essential ingredients in common. They both propagate the idea that Jews are intimately connected with evil. This seems to have its origins in pre-Vatican II Church teachings about Jews as eternally cursed by deicide – hence the use of "Jew" as invective.

Another element common to many forms of modem antisemitism is a product of recent Jewish history. The assimilated Jews became the epitome of the disguised alien. That is why in present-day Poland, where Jews more often than not are mythical figures, antisemitism is concrete as well as abstract. Antisemitic arguments are directed not only against certain activists of the opposition but also against some who are connected with the government. Among these are; the universally hated government spokesperson, Jerzy Urban, well-known journalists like Krzysztof Teodor Toeplitz and Daniel Passent[16], and noted critic Artur Sandauer[17], all of whom at one time were independent minded but now try their best to provide sophisticated arguments in support of the military government. All of them are more or less Jewish (by origin) – although this is not essential. For example there is widespread belief that Mieczyslaw Rakowski[18] is also a Jew.

16 Important liberal journalists, still active in broadly left wing politics. Passent was also the Polish ambassador to Latin America. He continues to be a columnist for the most important weekly *Polityka*.

17 An important independent critic, usually far from politics, promoter in France and in the West of outstanding Polish pre-war writers, like Bruno Schulz and Witold Gombrowicz. He survived a ghetto during the war.

18 A liberal communist and the last head of the communist party in Poland; not Jewish.

While both hostility and empathy towards Jews are clearly visible in Poland, it should be stressed that in general the "Jewish problem" in contemporary Polish life is a secondary issue. It should also be understood that even those described as "active" antisemites are only intellectually so (after all, they only talk). But from my perspective antisemitism, whether "active" or latent, seems to be more frequent than sympathy toward the Jews. On the other hand, I believe that the part of the younger generation which will constitute the Polish intellectual elite does feel empathy for the Jews. It is impossible, however, to tell whether these people will eventually form the political elite. One can only hope.[19]

[19] Interestingly, the hopes proved both fulfilled and dashed. The elite did emerge and is important in Poland, but at the same time groups with no openness to Jews, and sometimes explicitly antisemitic, have become increasingly influential.

Impact Of The Shoah On The Thinking Of Polish Jews After World War II

Note

Originally presented as a paper at a conference at Yeshiva University in 2000, the text that has served as the basis for the present chapter was published in *Contested Memories. Poles and Jews during the Holocaust and Its Aftermath* (ed. Joshua D. Zimmerman), Rutgers University Press, New Brunswick 2003.

0. Introduction

Post-war Poland is, roughly, my time and my place. I did not choose the place and time of birth – who did? – but it is my place, with its good and bad features. I have actively participated in Jewish life since1989 and to some extent in the 1980s. Before starting my journey to Jewish involvement while I was in my 20s in the 1970s, I belonged to the category of completely assimilated, non-Jewish Jews. This category is crucial for any attempt to understand the post-war Polish Jewish condition.

In the following pages, I shall consider the impact of the Shoah, an impossible task. It is, in one word, overwhelming. And for two reasons: the obvious Jewish one, and the less well-understood Polish one. When I was young, memory of the war was a dominant theme in Polish society. For decades films and most works of fiction were about the war. In contemporary Poland, one need only say "the war" to refer to World War II. And for Polish Jews of all categories, the war has been even more of a watershed. We have been living in the shadow of the Shoah, which has had direct consequences (devastation, a dramatic decline in Jewish numbers, changes in the ownership of property) and indirect ones (whereby, for example, its memory could easily lead to an approval of communism). Its most lasting psychological consequence is the fear of oppression and murder transmitted unwillingly to subsequent generations. That fear has contributed more than anything else to the hiding of one's Jewish roots in postwar Poland. Another long-term effect of the Shoah is how foreigners have viewed Polish Jewry; for foreign Jews, Poland has become a huge Jewish cemetery and nothing more. Let me stress at once that despite this harsh legacy, today's Jewish community in Poland is not some half-real remnant bound to the dead. We are as real and as future-oriented as other Jewish communities around the world.

Let us begin with the complex question of numbers. It is impossible to know precisely how many Jews were living in Poland during various periods in postwar Poland, or the size of today's community. The problem stems from the difficult question of who should be counted as "Jewish." Do we include marginally Jewish Jews? Do we include non-halakhic Jews (Jewish fathers only), and do we include Catholics of Jewish origin – or at least those among them who have some Jewish feelings?[1] Rather than trying to address all the ques-

1 Contrary to standard approaches, I believe that in the Polish context Catholics of Jewish origin should not be excluded because sometimes their children choose to come back to the Jewish fold.

tions I shall focus on the category of "marginal Jews", divided into three types: (1) "non-Jewish", or completely assimilated Jews who have no connection to Jewish life, (2) hidden Jews who have not yet, or may never, "come out of the closet," so to speak, (3) and communist Jews. On the basis of my experiences, I believe, as do quite a few of my friends, that in Poland today, there are many more marginal Jews than official members of Jewish organizations.[2] That is why there is no way to know the true number of Jews in Poland, as most hidden and assimilated Jews have chosen not to join Jewish organizations and are not counted. Therefore, I claim that nobody really knows the answer to the question of the size of Poland's Jewish population. The standard estimates of between 5,000 and 10,000 are misleading. While unregistered Jews are difficult to find and count in every country, this is particularly the case in Poland.

1. Polish Jews in the Immediate Post-War Years

The first post-war years witnessed a rather complex picture. It was the period of the post-Shoah shock, the still fresh awareness of the losses. All Jews were survivors. They were on the move. People were coming back from hiding, from camps, from Russia. Few were able to resettle in their homes: for two or three years Gentiles had lived there, and the new residents were not ready to give up their new houses. Because of that some Jews were murdered and thousands had to escape. In addition to antisemitism, Jews were subjects of a more general disorder: the whole country was re-emerging from chaos, affected by a radical change of borders, and population transfers of millions.

How many Jews were there? Those who survived in German-occupied Poland were joined by those who returned from Russia. By

[2] People who believe this way include some foreigners, such as Rabbi Michael Schudrich, who know Polish realities.

July 1, 1946, 243,926 persons had registered with the Central Committee of Polish Jews (CKŻP), a figure which does not take into account those Jews who never registered with Jewish organizations.[3] All statistics about the postwar Jewish population thus contain only a partial picture, leaving out many from among the marginal Jews as well as those Catholic converts. If all are taken into account we arrive, it seems to me, at the figure of well over 300,000 Jews. Not a small figure by many standards, even if a mere 10% of the pre-war Jewish population. And the number of Jews staying in Poland was steadily decreasing.

Emigration, which was a major phenomenon during the immediate post-war years, was caused by several elements: the memories of the tragedy, the feeling that Poland had become a huge Jewish cemetery, the fear of antisemitism, and Zionism. A major stimulus for emigration, or even escape, was provided by the most sinister event of that time, the infamous pogrom in Kielce, on July 4, 1946, when 42 Jews were killed by soldiers and a mob, which gathered when rumours of a ritual murder had been circulated.

The Jewish community, which reached its peak in the summer of 1946, remained substantial even after the massive post-Kielce and Zionist emigration waves.[4] In 1949, close to 100,000 Jews were registered in Poland on the occasion of the distribution of matzo for Pesach.[5]

Despite large-scale emigration, the period 1945-1949 was marked by a vibrant reconstruction of Jewish life. In 1946, the Joint supported 278 educational institutions with 20,631 students.[6] While only a frac-

3 Józef Adelson, "W Polsce zwanej ludową", *Najnowsze dzieje Żydów w Polsce* (ed. by Jerzy Tomaszewski), PWN, Warsaw 1993, 398.

4 In 1944-1947, the Zionist network Bericha facilitated the emigration of 70,000-140,000 Jews from Poland. See Adelson, 413, Alina Cała and Helena Datner *Dzieje Żydów w Polsce 1944-1968, Teksty Źródłowe*, ŻIH, Warszawa 1997, 168.

5 Adelson, 421.

6 Zofia Borzymińska, Rafał Żebrowski *Po-lin. Kultura Żydów polskich w XX wieku*, Amarant, Warszawa 1993, 309.

tion of Polish Jews embraced religious life at the time, there were still eighty communities with twenty-five rabbis in 1947.[7] Most social, educational, and cultural activities were conducted under the auspices of the predominantly secular left-wing CKŻP. The watchword was so-called 'produktywizacja', that is, teaching Jews skills needed in industry.

Despite relatively high support for the Communist Party, Jews and Jewish institutions suffered from communism as much as anyone else. Stalinist totalitarianism affected Jewish life as much as other sectors of Poland. In 1949-1950, all non-communist political parties were banned in Poland, including Jewish ones. All Jewish institutions – from schools to theatres – were nationalized while the borders were sealed, putting a halt to emigration.[8]

With the liberalization in the Soviet Union and Poland beginning in 1956, a new wave of immigrants reached Poland. Among those thousands of Polish citizens who returned to Poland from Russia there were 18,000 Polish Jews.[9] But even after Stalin's death in 1953 and the end to the terror, freedom was not granted in the late 1950s and 1960s. Despite the lack of freedoms, six state Jewish elementary schools and three Jewish high schools (all in Polish),[10] continued to function until 1967, as well as organized activities for Jewish youth such as Jewish scouting and Jewish summer camps. In addition, the Yiddish Theatre continued to be active in Warsaw. In the 1960s, the youth clubs of the communist-dominated Cultural Social Association of Jews in Poland were active and some of their members were involved in dissident activities.

Due to continued emigration, particularly in the period 1957-1958, the Jewish population continued to shrink. By 1961, the official Jewish population of Poland was 45,000.[11] We should nonethe-

[7] Borzymińska and Żebrowski, 307.
[8] Adelson, 477, Cała & Datner, 88, 224.
[9] Borzymińska and Żebrowski, 321.
[10] Borzymińska and Żebrowski, 322.
[11] Borzymińska and Żebrowski, 321.

less take into account the probability that the number of unaffiliated Jews (including those marginally Jewish, and their children) was comparable to (and perhaps higher than) the number of official members of the Jewish community.

2. 1967-1969: Official Antisemitism, Forced Emigration

The 1967 Six Day War gave rise to a so-called "anti-Zionist campaign" in Poland. The peak of this campaign coincided with the protests of students and intellectuals who demanded more freedom; the protest movement was repressed, and anti-Polish Zionist agitators were accused of manipulating students. The state-controlled media preached antisemitism. For a few months in factories, in the army, in state offices, and in universities, communist activists pointed out Jews whom they condemned as disloyal, pro-Israel, or anti-social. Sometimes they attacked non-Jews who looked Jewish or had Jewish sounding names. The difference between Socialism and National Socialism was blurred in the eyes of Jews.

The antisemitic propaganda of 1968 was without parallel in postwar Europe, as were the resulting purges and the consequent emigration of a majority of Polish Jews. The direct responsibility rests on the ruling communists but the significance of that antisemitic, anti-liberal and anti-intellectual campaign can be seen – to use the phrase of Adam Michnik – in the attempt to incorporate Polish extreme right wing traditions in order bring legitimacy to communist rule. About 15,000 Jews left Poland officially, and were forced to renounce their Polish citizenship.[12] Many left for Sweden and Denmark, where they received state assistance as refugees. Others went to Israel,[13] the United States, or other Western countries. It was

[12] Dariusz Stola, *Kampania antysyjonistyczna w Polsce 1967-1968*, ISPPAN, Warszawa 2000, 213. (There exists an abbreviated English version of this work: *Anti-Zionist Campaign in Poland 1967-1968*, American Jewish Committee, New York 1999.)

[13] About 28% of all Jewish emigrants of that period; see Stola, 214.

during the 1968 antisemitic campaign that some young citizens of Poland learned about their Jewish origin for the first time when their parents suddenly announced, "We are Jews and can't stand the antisemitic campaign. We're going to emigrate".

3. 1970-1989, after the Last Exodus: Decline and Independent Initiatives

The antisemitic propaganda of 1968 ceased after a few months. But it permanently changed the lives of Polish Jews, both those who emigrated and those of us who remained in Poland. For it was only after 1968 that I realized that we belonged to one group, and that Jewishness can be important, contrary to what my parents believed. Many other Polish Jews were like them, a good number of whom were communists who raised completely de-Judaized children, not infrequently in mixed marriages. Yet the fear and insecurity connected with Jewishness was often passed to the next generation. The parents transmitted to their children the feeling that Jewishness was irrelevant, obsolete, and that antisemitism was the only real dimension of being Jewish.

In 1968 I participated in the protest movement. I must stress that the "March 1968 events", despite the antisemitism, were shared by people like me and by the Catholic intelligentsia, which was also attacked for, among other things, being manipulated by Zionists. Although it is difficult now to believe, during the March 1968 events, all students, with the exception of official communists, protested against antisemitism. The bond created then remains alive even today.

After 1968, Jewish life in Poland seemed to be slowly coming to an end. Jewish schools disappeared and intellectual activities ceased. Some older Jews still met in order to speak Yiddish but that language too was disappearing. Neither Yiddish nor the domination of communists in Jewish institutions was attractive to the younger generation of Jews. The Yiddish Theatre in Warsaw had a very small audience that could understand the play without a Polish translation. In practice, the theatre began to function as a museum after 1968. Since the government controlled Jewish organizations, their leadership publicly supported the official anti-Zionist policy.

During this period, Jewish topics were nonexistent in official cultural life. Although underground, uncensored publications of the1980s helped to break the taboo, their influence was limited. At the same time, in private semi-clandestine groups, some children of assimilated Jews began to explore their Jewish roots and to look for Jewish knowledge. My own group, active from the late 1970s, was called – in the spirit of Polish conspiratorial traditions – the Jewish Flying University. With no or minimal contact with the organized Jewish community, we learned, discussed, and eventually celebrated Jewish holidays.

Many of us who began exploring our Jewish roots were also involved in Polish national life during the dissident period of the 1970s, and the eruption of 1980. Most young Jews and quite a few of the older generation shared the enthusiasm of the initial "Solidarność" movement. To many it was like returning from an "internal emigration," initiated by the 1968 campaign. The liberalization of 1980-81 was helpful to those seeking their Jewish identity because, for the first time since the late 1940s, many articles and books on Jewish topics were published, such as accounts of the Kielce pogrom.[14] The public was hungry. I was therefore not really surprised that my wife's book of photographs of Jewish cemeteries became a bestseller in the 1980s.[15] These developments of the early 1980s later bore fruit in organized Jewish life.

14 For example, in 1981, Krystyna Kersten's first article on Kielce pogrom appeared, "Kielce – 4 lipiec 1946 r.," *Tygodnik Solidarność* 36 (4 Dec. 1981). For other examples, and for the significance of the Solidarity period, see Chapter 6.

15 Monika Krajewska, *Czas Kamieni*, Interpress, 1982, appeared in Polish, English, German, and French. An improved version, *A Tribe of Stones*, was published in 1993, only in English.

4. Renewal: Jewish Life in Post-communist Poland

The small renaissance of organized Jewish life began on the eve of the fall of communism when, in 1988, the New York-based Ronald S. Lauder Foundation inaugurated its educational summer camps. Freedom and educational possibilities have made possible the emergence of new Jewish institutions since 1989, and revitalization of some old ones, notably the Union of Jewish Religious Communities. While the formally Orthodox character is maintained, women have been granted equal rights in institutional life, and a woman, the sociologist Helena Datner, was president of the Warsaw Community from 1998 to 2001. Also, the criteria for membership have been liberalized in most communities: either Jewish ancestry or conversion is accepted In some communities a new generation of leaders is present, partly from among those who participated in the independent Jewish activities in the 1980s. There are some young Jews who see Jewishness as primarily religious, but the majority, young and old alike, are far from religion.

After 1968, no Jewish schools existed, and almost no Jewish education was offered in Poland. But Jewish education was revived in the 1990s with the formation of a Jewish kindergarten and Jewish elementary school in Warsaw, a Jewish elementary school in Wrocław, and on-going educational activities, all of them supported by the Lauder Foundation. The combined membership in all the schools is well over 200 students, some of them without Jewish roots. This leads to a natural involvement in Jewish life of some of the children of assimilated Jews. Due to involvement in the new Jewish schools, the parents of those students are also beginning to learn Jewish traditions.

In sharp contrast to the decades of communist Poland, information on Judaism and Jewish history is now readily available. Scores of books have been translated, some written by local authors. There are also periodical publications like the bi-weekly *Dos yiddishe vort*, in Polish and Yiddish, the monthly *Midrasz*, in Polish; there have been various bulletins, and for several years an irregular youth magazine *Jidele* appeared, all in Polish. In addition, the Jewish Historical Institute in Warsaw publishes a scholarly journal.

Among the new institutions there is the Union of Jewish Students and the Association of Jewish Combatants. Other institutions, like the Social-Cultural Association of Jews in Poland (TSKŻ), continue their cultural activities, although the Yiddish language, which was formerly its hallmark, is not known to the post-war generations. Both the old and the new institutions get support from the JDC, or the Joint. Financial self-sufficiency is not yet in sight. This may become a possibility only when successful professionals and business people decide to join the organizations in larger numbers. Things can also improve due to the on-going restitution of former Jewish communal property.

Restitution means the return of some property to eight religious communities. In the parts of Poland where no communities exist, the restitution is handled by a foundation, created jointly by the Union of Jewish Communities and the World Jewish Restitution Organization. Misunderstandings concerning the prospects of the restitution are widespread. Contrary to the vision of many foreigners it will never bring enough money to take proper care of over one thousand Jewish cemeteries in Poland. Still, the communities will have their own sources of funding, and this proves to be a mixed blessing. The smell of money can attract people who do not otherwise care about Jewishness, and some of them may try to gain control of the situation in anticipation of financial benefit. This danger has already been apparent. This can push off the *pintele Yiden*, non-Jewish Jews with a Jewish spark in their hearts, even further from the organized Jewish life.

Marginal Jews constitute the main pool of potential new members of organized Jewish life. Also, input can be made by American and other foreign Jews who live in Warsaw and in some other Polish cities working for foreign companies. Among them are emigrants who left in 1968-69 as young people, and now do business in Poland. Their impact upon organized Jewish life until now has been minimal. The notable exception is the *Beit Warszawa* association, which functions to some extent as a Reform congregation in Warsaw. It is also conceivable that some Jews from the former Soviet Union, who have come to do business in Poland, can join. In addition, Judaism is attractive to some non-Jews, as is the case everywhere else in the Western world. It is, however, only the Polish non-Jewish Jews, or Poles of Jewish origin, who can provide the membership that is necessary for the continuation of Polish Jewish life.

5. Marginal Jews Today

Perhaps the main characteristic of the re-emerging community is an almost complete generation gap. Old members of Jewish organizations have children who are unaffiliated even when they live in Poland (although they often live abroad). Those members who were born after the war have parents who do not belong to any Jewish organization. Those younger ones, who are culturally Polish, come from the pool of marginal Jews, or Poles of Jewish origin.

In Poland we have hundreds, and thousands, and possibly dozens of thousands of so-called hidden Jews. Their number will remain unknown. During the war to survive meant to hide one's Jewishness efficiently. It was literally a matter of life and death. After the war Jewishness could mean danger. Moreover, it was simpler not to disclose Jewish origins if one sought a career in the Polish communist regime.

So a lot of Jews remained hidden – some until 1968, some until today. They often intermarried, and sometimes did not tell their spouse about their ancestry. In the meantime, these hidden Jews had children who had no knowledge of their Jewish ancestry. If 1968 did not provide sufficient stimulus to re-embrace some Jewish identity, their children and grandchildren are probably still unaware of their roots. Some became extremely committed and devout Catholics.

An example will be instructive. In the early 1990s a Jewish friend in his forties bought an apartment in Warsaw. Soon it turned out that the woman living next door was Jewish, but had been raised Catholic and had only recently learned about her parents' origins. The neighbour's Christian faith was thus shaken, but meanwhile her mother had become an even more devout Catholic. The neighbour's husband hesitated to inform his family about his wife's revelation of Jewish origins out of fear of antisemitism. But when he ended up telling his family, he learned that his father was Jewish. My friend also learned that another new neighbour of his was Jewish but was so shy and inhibited that he preferred not to speak to anybody. In befriending a resident from the floor above, my friend, in hearing a wartime childhood story, suspected that she too was born to a Jewish family. While all these neighbours continue their ways and have refrained from involvement in Jewish life, my friend could not help but feel that he unexpectedly came to live in a place with some Jewish vibrations.

One initiative to reach marginal Jews in Poland has been the Jewish Hotline service. The Jewish Hotline was formed in 1996 by the Jewish Forum, a Warsaw circle of Jewish professionals who have acquired a strong Jewish identity. Some of us had been active since our days in the Jewish Flying University, back in the late 1970s, when our first meetings resembled group therapy sessions. At that time, we had to express and to try to overcome deep-seated emotions connected with Jewishness: uncertainty, shame, and above all, fear. We were learning how to say "I'm Jewish" in a casual way.

Having struggled with the complexities of our Jewish identities and the exploration of Jewish roots, we decided to establish a Jewish hotline in Warsaw, which was in operation every Thursday evening for anyone who wanted to discuss anonymously problems related to Jewish roots, self-identity and how this affected their relations with spouses, children, parents, or colleagues. The conversations were confidential, revealed to nobody. We also provided valuable information on Jewish institutions. People kept calling the one afternoon-per-week hotline from October 1996 to 2001. Sometime in 2002 the interest grew smaller and we discontinued the service. About one third of the phone calls were from individuals who were trying to come to terms with the challenge of Jewishness. Among them were elderly people who felt uneasy that while making careers they completely abandoned their pre-war Jewish upbringing and now felt their children should know something; but how to tell them? We could reassure them that their situation was rather typical. There were also young people who felt that a family secret pointed to Jewish origins (for example, nothing was known about a caller's mother's pre-war past, and no family has survived). We could confirm to such callers that it was likely the mother was of Jewish origin, but to know for sure it would be best to talk with her. The most dramatic calls were those by persons in their fifties who recently discovered that they had been Jewish babies rescued and raised during the war by Polish Catholic families as their own.

In our leaflet one reads, among other things, the following:

Do you have Jewish roots?

Is it your problem? Or is it your secret? And perhaps your passion, pride, and hope?

Are you ashamed because you are of Jewish origin? Are you afraid? Do you happen to hide it? Maybe you don't know what to tell your spouse or your colleagues, your boyfriend or girlfriend? Possibly, you don't know what you should tell your children? How to address the topic in your office? And when?

Perhaps you feel a pride or a bond with other Jews, but you don't know how to express it? Or you regret that you have been told so little about your Jewish ancestors? And maybe you would like to meet other Jews but you have no opportunity? Perhaps the presence of other Jews makes you feel uncomfortable? Maybe you think that antisemites are not completely wrong?

Perhaps you don't know how to respond to antisemitism? And maybe you are convinced that what really matters are universal problems and not particular dilemmas of Jews? Do you feel that Jewishness doesn't matter to you, and you are irritated that others link you to it? Perhaps the synagogue is alien to you, and the church seems familiar? Possibly, you fear that if you admitted the importance of Jewishness you would lose your Polish identity?

You don't have to face such problems alone!

Support groups are the natural next step for those who want to discuss the meaning of Jewish identity in contemporary Poland, and problems resulting from it with people who have similar experiences. A few groups were organized, mostly in cooperation with an American psychologist, partly through advertisements ("The Broken Chain" project), and partly for those who called the hotline and were interested.

The Jewish Hotline provoked sarcastic criticism. Since it was listed in some major newspapers alongside hotlines for battered wives, or those infected with AIDS, our critics asked "Is Jewishness an illness?" Well, of course not, but when it constitutes a hidden and unexplored aspect of one's personality it causes psychological problems similar to those suffered by gays or people with AIDS.

What has caused Jews to hide their identity in Poland? Briefly, World War II, and communism. The war was, as mentioned above, the major cause. Among its most afflicted victims were children. Few survived. For them a very interesting unique organization has been formed in Poland: the "Association of Hidden Children of the Holocaust" consisting of individuals who were Jewish children in Poland during the war and have lived in Poland ever since. Having begun with a few individuals they now have hundreds of members. Some of them are university professors; others are uneducated women who married in the village in which they were hiding. Quite a few of the members are Catholic. They have, however, something very deep in common, due to their childhood experiences.

6. Communism

As mentioned earlier, the impact of communism on Jewish life has been very strong: anti-communist Jews mostly emigrated, pro-communist Jews were very active, and Jewish institutions were completely controlled by communists. Most of the communist Jews were far from any Jewish involvement. Not a few were hiding their Jewishness. The impact of communism was that Jews, from all sections of the community, learned to play down their Jewishness. To some, it was a continuation of the attitude adopted during the war. To give a simple but telling example, hardly any baby boys were circumcised in post-war Poland. In fact, it was only in the 1990s that dozens of us, middle aged and young Polish Jews, were finally circumcised.

World War II was a watershed for Polish Jews. It proved to them that the traditional European approaches to the "Jewish problem" lead to catastrophe. If democracy leads to Hitler, only radically new social solutions can be accepted. They went in two opposite directions. One was escape from Europe, either to Israel, America, or Australia. Europe, and especially Poland, was a cemetery, a devastated, hopeless, and always dangerous land. The other way was to engage in a revolutionary rebuilding of Poland or other nations. Zionists combined both solutions.

The Jews who chose to remain in Poland for ideological reasons felt that radical Jewish solutions, like Zionism, were not for them, because those proposals emphasized Jewishness against all the other elements of their identity. To them the communist vision of a "classless" society seemed worth trying. Logically, even the deeply Jewish among the communists did not introduce their children to Jewish traditions. For communists there was no future for Jews. Religious and ethnic differences were doomed to disappear. This vision of the irrelevance of Judaism and of the harmfulness of any Jewish distinctiveness influenced deeply not only communist Jews but also other non-Jewish Jews. Normal life in the new society had no place for Jewish involvement other than, perhaps, a sentimental attitude to Yiddish. It was natural for them to Polonize surnames, or to retain the Christian names adopted during the war. However, what to them was the repudiation of Judaism to others looked like concealment of their true identity. And sometimes it was just that.

The concealment of Jewish origins reinforced the antisemitic conviction that hidden Jews rule Poland. I believe that, independently of the need to denounce and ridicule this view, it is necessary to face the problem of the role of Jewish communists both in Poland and in other countries.

7. Communist Jews

There were two categories of Jewish communists in post-war Poland; the minority who were acting among Jews, and the majority who were active at the national level. The latter were very visible, the more so because Poles were not used to the idea that Jews could have equal opportunities in the state bureaucracy. Whatever the historical background and perceptions of the general population, the fact remains that Jews, admittedly non-committed Jews and often "non-Jewish" Jews, were numerous and influential in the communist elite in post-war Poland.

In my view, this constitutes a moral challenge for us Jews. Of course, antisemites exaggerate and abuse the numbers to such a degree that it is hard to accept that there is a genuine problem here.

communists or even leftists never constituted a majority among Jews in general. Yet in post-war Poland, when most Jews emigrated, among the remaining ones communists were numerous, and certainly most visible. This is a great drama of post-war Jewish Poland: from outside one saw the flow of Jewish refugees, from inside – the numerous Jews in the power elite. Those Jews participated actively in the system of oppression. I am saying this with full awareness that there were idealists among them whose acceptance of communism was initially caused by noble motives. Yet while their counterparts in the West remained idealist theoretical radicals, those in Poland or other East European countries became functionaries of the state terror. I believe that this is a reason for Jews to feel shame. Of course, I am not saying that only Jews should be morally responsible.

My point is simple but rarely accepted: (a) communism belongs also to the history of Jews, not just to the history of Russia, Poland, etc. (b) In the middle of our century, in the heart of Europe, Jews were not only victims but also victimizers. (c) To some Jews, communism was a quasi-religion.[16]

8. The Need for a Normal Existence

Polish Jews in Poland are not uniform. They range from Orthodox to (more numerous) liberal to (even more numerous) anti-religious, from publicly involved to (many more) privately involved to (even more numerous) hidden Jews. There exist, however, common elements. The most obvious is fear of antisemitism. Virtually all Polish Jews feel that antisemitism is widespread and that sensitivity of Poles to Jewish concerns is low. This is despite the presence of individuals and groups who have good will, who are open to Jewish experiences and opposed to antisemitism, and despite the fact that our re-

[16] A much more comprehensive presentation of this position is contained in the ten theses on Jews and communism presented in Chapter 4.

lations with the government are good. In the late 1990s the number of antisemitic incidents increased. With the 1998 Auschwitz crosses controversy, which was ultimately resolved when the crosses, with the exception of the so-called Papal cross, were removed by government order in May 1999, extreme antisemitism has become more visible and the voices of its leaders have been quoted in the mainstream media. In the new millennium antisemitism has not grown, in happy contrast to much of Western Europe. However, we have had a new reason for the expression of anti-Jewish attitudes. Previously, most tensions relating to Jews concerned interpretations of history and symbols. The recent very concrete problem of restoring property to the Jewish community; property lost during the German occupation or from communist confiscations, has raised new emotions. Jewish claims are widely met with particular suspicion.

At the same time a positive interest in Jewish history and culture is also part of Polish reality. Much more than in the past, Jewish history is now being studied at universities, in schools and through museums. A most notable event attracting both affiliated and assimilated Jews, though not intended specifically for them, is the remarkable annual international festival of Jewish culture in Krakow. It includes top quality art exhibitions, theatre performances, movies, lectures, craft workshops, and especially concerts of cantors, orchestras, klezmer bands, and singers. There is more to this than just cultural interest. Several years ago it was fashionable to be Jewish in Poland. We can still feel the legacy of that fashion. This is important because in such an atmosphere it is easier for marginal Jews to admit their Jewishness.

9. The Role of Auschwitz

We all live in the shadow of the Shoah. At the same time most of us are angry with foreigners who want to reduce our lives to a Shoah-dominated existence. We live normal lives, and we look to the future, not to the past. And yet I admit that Auschwitz is an essential point of reference for Polish Jews. Moreover, it is in some sense, the most important, and certainly the best known internationally, site in Poland. It has assumed symbolic power recognized by virtually everyone in the world. And it has a sinister power: it has been creating controversies. These include the presence of Carmelite nuns just outside the camp's barbed wire in the 1980s, and later in connection with the presence of religious symbols, especially crosses, at the same place. We, Polish Jews, against our intentions, live on the battlefront, attacked by Jewish radicals from abroad and by militant Catholics in Poland. This is a burden. But it is also a challenge.[17]

One consequence of the peculiarities of contemporary Polish Jewry is that marginal Jews are not left alone. They are forced to address such problems, and even if this means opposing Jewish activists, or objecting to the chauvinistic elements in the March of the Living program, they still have to ponder what being Jewish means to them.

10. A Future for Polish Jews?

Despite all these peculiarities, our Jewish community is slowly becoming more and more like Western communities. This means cultural assimilation, participating in national life, and familiarity with Christianity. A process of *de-assimilation* has begun. This is a novelty in the history of Jews in Poland. While in the nineteenth century and in the first half of the twentieth century more and more Jews assimilated to the majority culture, aspired to rootedness in it, and were losing their Jewish commitments, I, like many other Jews in today's Poland, have regained the Jewish identity and knowledge that

[17] Some philosophical problems connected to the symbolism of Auschwitz are considered in Chapter 1.

my parents did not pass on. Unlike our ancestors, we do not need to aspire to being Polish, because we have been raised Polish. We can be as Polish and Jewish as English Jews are English and Jewish. Indeed, I believe that we are as much Polish and Jewish as English Jews are English and Jewish (I wouldn't dare to say, "as American Jews are American and Jewish"). In this respect Poland is also on its way to joining Europe, and the situation of Polish Jews can be a good measure of the remaining distance.

Assimilation has reached its limits. We have lost so many Jews because of it. But now de-assimilation has been growing. Interestingly, this de-assimilation in most cases does not mean de-Polonization. With the exception of a few who have become very Orthodox and often eventually leave Poland, most Jews in Poland remain involved in Polish life. The days of a specific Jewish nation speaking its own language are gone (in no Polish family is Yiddish the language of communication). Meanwhile, we can measure our success by the rate of appearance of problems that plague Western Jewish communities. Thus one must ponder the role of religion in a predominantly secular world, the strength of assimilation, or the need to find answers to the question, "Why be Jewish?"

Being Jewish in Poland is more and more voluntary. One can stop, in practice, being Jewish, and on the other hand, one can become Jewish. Neither of the two processes is easy but they are happening. I hope that the net result of all the developments will be positive. I feel that if the Jewish community disappeared from Poland it would be tragic not just for me but also for Poland, for Jews everywhere, and for the world. To us, Polish Jews, even more than to others, one can direct the famous motto of Emil Fackenheim; that if we disappeared it would be a posthumous victory for Hitler.

The Catholic Church, The Polish Church, And The Jews

Note

The present chapter surveys the positive changes in the official Catholic teachings about Jews and Judaism, and relates them to the situation in Poland. This essay is based on a lecture I gave at a meeting in Warsaw, in 2000. During the meeting I proposed a top level ceremony at the place of the massacre in Jedwabne with the participation of "3 P", or the President, the Prime Minister and the Primate. An expanded text of the lecture was published in Polish, under the title "Teszuwa", in the Catholic monthly *Więź* (2/2001, 29-45). At the same time, the English version was prepared and published in Sweden in the book edited by Michał Bron Jr, *Jews and Christians in Dialogue II: Identity – Tolerance – Understanding*, Almquist & Wiksell International, Stockholm 2001, 188-201.

We all, Jews, Christians, and the rest of us, need *teshuvah* (repentance, in Hebrew), that is turning away from sins. But teshuvah is usually a process rather than a single act. The Jewish tradition requires us to repent and also to accept the repentance of those who have harmed us. If we apply this to interfaith relations between

Christians and Jews we should ask first whether there is a teshuvah of the Church, and if so, are Jews accepting it?

I do not mean that Jews are only victims, who are never guilty, and that Christians have never been victims of Jews. Specifically, there were Jews (though never only Jews) among the atheist regimes that persecuted Churches (and, for that matter, the Synagogue, too). Still, there has been a lack of balance: incomparably more often Jews were victims of Christians than *vice versa*. And in addition, Jews were sometimes victimized not just by Christians but by the teachings and actions of the Church, while no Jewish institutions, as opposed to individual Jews, were victimizing Christians. That is why it seems fair to put emphasis on the repentance of the Church and on the reactions of Jews.

1. The *teshuvah* of the Church

The last forty years have witnessed a great reorientation of the Catholic Church, as well as of many Protestant ones. Point 4 of the "*Nostra Aetate*" declaration of the Second Vatican Council, issued in 1965, removed from the official Church instruction the so-called "teaching of contempt". For centuries Jews had been seen as blind, spiritually inferior, guilty of deicide, damned, worthy of discrimination that would show their error; the Church had been seen as the new Israel that replaced the old one, the Jews.

In modern times, since the French revolution, we have witnessed the stress on individual choice, the gradual emancipation of much of Western social life from direct rule of religion, the growing secularization, and the triumph of the concept of human rights and human equality. All these elements contributed to the change of Christian-Jewish relations. The most powerful stimulus for change came, however, from the Shoah. It was shocking that in the middle of Christian Europe arouse a scheme to murder all

Jews. Although Hitler was not acting in the name of Christianity, his ideology was a culmination of the tradition, perpetuated by the Church, to perceive Jews as devils.

In Poland, the nation most hurt by World War II, the shock was not comparable to the Western perceptions: the Shoah was seen as a crime committed by the Germans, and the challenge to Christianity, let alone a Christian guilt, was ignored. And yet the Polish Church has been participating in the general reorientation. Growing number of Polish Catholics accept the new teaching, and the Church's teshuvah.

The milestones on the way to the new teaching are the already mentioned declaration "*Nostra Aetate*" of 1965, and the Vatican documents of 1974 and 1985, describing its implementation.[1] They stress the common roots, and proclaim the abandonment of "substitution theology". They teach that the Church has not replaced Israel; that the covenant with Jews is irrevocable, and the presence of Jews in the land of Israel is "a sign". John Paul II has extended this, calling antisemitism a sin, and referring to Jews as "elder brothers", during his historic visit to the synagogue in Rome in 1986. Few people outside Poland know that this phrase, which has justly become famous, was probably taken from the Polish Romantic poet Adam Mickiewicz, whose works the Pope learned in school at Polish literature lessons. This is a reason for pride for us Poles.

A new phase of the process of teshuvah was initiated by John Paul II in his letter "*Tertio Millenio Advenniente*" of 1994. The appeal for an examination of conscience pointed also to antisemitism. As a consequence, there was, first, the 1997 symposium on "roots of anti-Judaism," and then, in March 1998, the Vatican's document "*We Remember: a Reflection on the Shoah*". This document, in which the term "teshuvah" is actually used, had been under preparation for 11 years.

[1] These were: *Guidelines and Suggestions for Implementing the Conciliar Declaration* Nostra Aetate (no. 4), Rome 1974, and *Notes on the Correct Way to Represent the Jews and Judaism in preaching and Catechesis in the Roman Catholic Church*, Rome 1985.

The document emphasizes the anti-Nazi statements of Christians; about the darker side it is only said that Christians did not always act in the way "followers of Christ" should. Thus, no answer is given to the question of co-responsibility – whether the Shoah was made easier by "anti-Jewish prejudice".

The next major text is a long document of December 1999 "*Memory and Reconciliation: the Church and the Faults of the Past.*" In addition to an analysis of the general question of responsibility for guilt of previous generations, the document recognizes the problem of forced conversions, and then, in point 5.4, summarizes the theses of "*We Remember*". The authors conclude that "the history of the relations between Jews and Christians is a tormented one … In effect, the balance of these relations over two thousand years has been quite negative."

The peak of the process of the "purification of memory" was reached in the unprecedented penitential liturgy by John Paul II on March 12, 2000. He confessed the sins of Christians, among them "sins against the people of Israel". He did it to God, in the presence of humans, and actually of millions TV-viewers. The Pope also declared the readiness to a "genuine brotherhood with the people of the Covenant." These motifs were also visible during his memorable visit to Israel, also in March 2000. It was clear that Israelis were moved by the Pope's attitude, about which only very few had had any idea.

Two more steps made by the Vatican, both taken in September 2000, must be mentioned here, though they seem to go in another direction. One is the statement by Cardinal Ratzinger "*Dominus Iesus: On the Unicity and Salvific Universality of Jesus Christ and the Church*", the other is the beatification of Pius IX. In the statement, Ratzinger wrote nothing about Judaism, and he clearly had other questions on his mind, but he stated strongly that there are no parallel ways to redemption, and the only one is through Jesus. Also, the Catholic

Church is described as the supreme religion. I know that one can interpret those claims either in a more ecumenical or in a more triumphalistic way. The language of the declaration suggested the latter, even though the Pope later said that no ecumenical achievement might be rejected.

Even more disturbing to Jews was the beatification of the Pope who in the mid-nineteenth century was behind the kidnapping of Edgaro Mortara, a Jewish child who had been baptized secretly by his nanny. This case has remained so far-reaching that one can't help but ask how to understand the words of the Council and the Pope that "the truth cannot impose itself except by virtue of its own truth."

The moral is clear: the process of teshuvah is meandering. Age-old problems return, like the teaching that there is no redemption "*extra Ecclesiam*", or that the value of Judaism is not comparable to that of Christianity. How are we to understand the conflicting messages? Some say that it is an application of the Catholic idea of confession: you ask forgiveness, and the slate is wiped clean. This interpretation may be unfair and vicious. One thing is sure: the admirable efforts by the Church to forge a new teaching about Jews are not a single act but a process, possibly a lengthy development.

2. Jewish Reactions

What were the Jewish responses to the teshuvah of the Church? According to Rabbi Michael Signer, we have witnessed a choreographic pattern:

First comes dialogue; then a statement from the Vatican Commission on Religious Relations with the Jews; and then the cacophony of voices from the Jewish community with some responding "Not enough!" and other responding "We have gone further on the journey. We shall continue."

Thus, for example, in *Nostra Aetate*, and its 1974 sequel, there was nothing on the Shoah or on the Jewish links to the Land of Israel. Some Jews complained about the new teaching of respect for Judaism, while others welcomed it. In a 1985 document the State of Israel was mentioned. But sceptics pointed to the lack of Vatican's normal diplomatic relations with Israel. They remembered the traditional hostility: Pius X told Theodore Herzl: "Jews have not recognized our Lord, therefore we cannot recognize the Jewish people.... Should the Jews manage to set foot on the once promised old-new land, the missionaries of the Church would stand prepared to baptize them." And yet in 1995 diplomatic relations were established. In the long run, the progress has been evident.

An official statement on the Shoah came even later. We must, however, remember John Paul's words on many occasions, first in 1979, during his first visit to Poland. To him the Holocaust was no abstraction but a part of his personal wartime experience. The 1998 document "*We remember*" and the 1999 document "*Memory and Reconciliation*" are not satisfactory because they do not touch the problem of "the silence of the Church" or the accusations against Pius XII. Generally speaking, the Church is absolved by the documents. To ask, as they do, whether "Christians gave all possible help" is not enough. The problem of how Christian teachings and practice in Europe prepared the ground for the Shoah is not treated, even though the existence of "anti-Jewish prejudice" is mentioned. Yet the two documents are valuable. They began an officially-sanctioned process of reflection, in which each problem can be faced.

The Pope's remarkable penitential service in March 2000 used very weak language. Antisemitism was mentioned without using either the term "antisemitism" or even the word "Jew". No specific event was mentioned. And yet those restrained words are of great importance. They urge contrition and appeal to ask for forgiveness and to forgive. This is difficult to every one of us, and needed by all of us. Some Jewish reactions were not positive, asking why the Shoah was not mentioned. But American associations of Conservative and Reform Rabbis (the Rabbinical Assembly and the Central Conference of American Rabbis), with a combined membership of 3,000, officially thanked the Pope for his message of respect for Judaism, for confessing the guilt, and for the seeking of forgiveness. The two organizations called upon their "rabbinic constituents to engage in intensified dialogue and fellowship with our Roman Catholic neighbours."

Despite all the reservations, one thing is certain. The Church has made exceptional, admirable progress. It has completely reoriented its official teachings; Jews, who used to be seen as a theological and social negative point of reference, have become partners. Despite all the meandering this is an astonishing accomplishment. How revolutionary it is can be seen in the fact that, unlike other statements of the Council, point 4 of *Nostra Aetate* makes no references to previous Church documents. Has there been anything comparable to that change of official stance? I doubt it. And the way John Paul II proposed and implemented the examination of conscience is unprecedented, and can serve as a model for all. As Rabbi Harold Schulweis said about this:

It is nothing less than heroic for any faith group to examine its darker side. How often in history, if ever, have the leaders of any faith publicly confessed its believers' transgressions and urged them to engage in an agonizing reappraisal of its words and deeds toward the people of another faith?

Having said this, I must point to a deep controversy that reappears all the time. In the introduction to the 1997 symposium Father Georges Cottier, "the Pope's theologian", mentioned "the contrast that exists between the holiness of the Church of Christ and the sin of its children." The matter does not look the same for someone outside the Church. The key to forgiveness lies, as said the Pope, in the understanding of guilt. What can the guilt of the Church be? For the Pope and the authors of the 1999 document, members of the Church can be guilty but not the Church as such. Traditionally, the Church cannot be tainted by sin. Only individual Christians, including priests, can be guilty. According to the John Paul II (as quoted in the "*Memory and Reconciliation*" 1.3),

Sin is … always personal, … situations of "social sin" … are always the result of "the accumulation and concentration of many personal sins".

This sounds convincing, at least to me. The problem arises, however, if from this point of view it is at all possible to point to the guilt of the official teaching of the Church. Of course, it was always formulated by individuals so they can be blamed, but it seems to me that the official teachings, presenting an essential truth, expressing the basics of the faith, are more than just errors of individuals.

It is beyond doubt that for centuries the Church was spreading "the teaching of contempt". It is not clear to me whether this fact can be admitted from the viewpoint adopted in the above mentioned documents. "*Memory and Reconciliation*" contains a sophisticated analysis of the difference between the activities of the Church as a community of faith, and those of it as an institution, especially in the era when the Church was ruling. It is right to ask whether it is not "too easy to judge people of the past by the conscience of today." (1.4). Also, I understand full well that it is important to distinguish the sinners in the Church from the Church as a whole, which "is maintained in holiness by the Holy Spirit." (3.2). What is more, I see here an analogy with the traditional Jewish vision of the mission of Israel; the holiness of the Church as God's gift that "guarantees the continuity of the mission of the People of God until the end of time" (3.2) corresponds to our vision of the holiness of Israel (despite important differences in details). No wonder: after all, the sources are the same. The traditional Jewish objection to this presentation of the Christian mission is that somebody is usurping the right to our mission. I believe this objection can be overcome. Moreover, I feel that the document can be instructive for Jews. After all we are struggling with an analogous problem: what is the relationship between the holiness of Israel and the typical lack of holiness of individual children of Israel? And yet, having said this, I cannot help but add that it was the Church as a whole that was a threat to Jews.

In fact, the traditional Jewish attitude to the Church was that the Church as such was dangerous, even though some of its members were friendly. This has changed, though not for all, and not everywhere. For example, I am ashamed that in Israeli schools nothing is taught about post-war developments in the Catholic Church. I just hope that the visit of John Paul II to Israel can change this.

3. A Jewish Declaration

Many Jewish leaders have been reluctant to accept the efforts of the Church. Too little, they say. Some representatives of the World Jewish Congress were making comments only about the steps that displeased Jews, like the projects to beatify or canonize Edith Stein, Pius XII, or Pius IX. This "negativism" provoked Cardinal Cassidy to say that it is perhaps better to do nothing than to be constantly criticized. I understand this, though the fact is that the recent elevation of Pius IX and the tone of Cardinal Ratzinger's statement have created difficulties for Jewish supporters of dialogue. Rabbi Toaff of Rome even decided to cancel his participation in the Day of Dialogue on October 3, 2000. I am sure, however, that the Autumn of 2000 has been dominated by another event, a very different Jewish response to the teshuvah of the Church.

Against this negativism, in September 2000 declaration "*Dabru emet*: a Jewish statement on Christians and Christianity" was published by 170 Rabbis and Jewish scholars, mainly from North America. It contains two messages. One, the Church's reorientation of attitude towards Jews is commended with no reservations; "it is time for Jews to learn about the efforts of Christians to honour Judaism." Two, an appeal to Jews is made: "it is time for Jews to reflect on what Judaism may now say about Christianity." To this effect the authors propose eight points. The Hebrew title means "tell the truth", and is quoted from the book of Zechariah 8:16. According to the declaration, the truth should be told about the positive aspects of Christianity from the Jewish perspective. Jews should overcome the perception of Christianity solely through the lens of "the teaching of contempt" and the discrimination against Jews. These well-known negative facts are virtually omitted in this text. I find this most appropriate. The signatories have proved that it is possible to rise above resentments. I am convinced that this is what is needed, which is not to say that the bad experiences may be forgotten.

The first four of the eight points result from the fact that Christianity and Judaism share the sources: the same God, the Hebrew Scripture, the Biblical vision of man in the image of the Creator, and the Biblically based understanding of the link of Jews to the Promised Land, or the Land of Israel. Between the two faiths there exists a bond, despite the differences. Of course, the differences are theologically essential: from the Jewish perspective it is unacceptable to describe God as a Trinity, to interpret Biblical texts as referring to Jesus, or to venerate icons (this brings to mind idolatry). Yet, there exists an equally essential deep connection. This is more than a family tie. It is of the utmost importance for Judaism that the fundamental Jewish categories – the God of Abraham, the Torah and the prophets, the Promised Land, the rejection of idolatry – all have been taught to hundreds of millions on our globe due to the Church, or rather the Churches.

The fifth point is that "Nazism was not a Christian phenomenon." The sixth is about the differences between the two traditions that "will not be settled until God redeems the entire world as promised in Scripture." Also, it makes the statement that while Jews serve God through Torah, "Christians know and serve God through Jesus Christ."

The seventh point is to comfort Jews. The authors admit the danger of religious and cultural assimilation, but they stress that friendly relations with Christians will not increase assimilation nor reduce traditional Jewish practice. The last point concerns the need of cooperation between Jews, Christians, and other faith communities for common good.

Points five and six are especially noteworthy. Critics say that the thesis that "Nazism was not a Christian phenomenon" suggests the innocence of the Church, though it was Christianity that prepared the ground for Nazism. Among the critics of this document are some like Rabbi James Rudin, advisor to the American Jewish Committee on interfaith relations, who agree with the remainder of the Statement but did not sign it because of what they perceive as a misleading approach to the connection of the Church to the Shoah. The answer of the "*Dabru emet*" supporters is that the declaration mentions the fact that the ground on which Nazism grew was prepared by Christianity but that "Nazism itself was not an inevitable outcome of Christianity." Opponents say, however, that we should talk about "the real Christianity" that did lead to Fascism and Nazism, rather than a detached "ideal Christianity".

I believe that this controversy points to a key problem: either you see mainly, or even exclusively, the "real Christianity" and the historical Church, or you see "the authentic Christianity", and its necessarily idealized attitudes. Which of the two we adopt, or in what proportion, determines our opinion about the thesis on Nazism, and on many other issues. Even in the Middle Ages, the reactions of Rabbis to the Christian cult of saints was mixed; some said that it was a specific form of relating, ultimately, to God, while others perceived an idolatrous cult.

Point six of the statement is of utmost importance: it puts the two religions on the same level. Christians are seen as deserving the same religious respect as do Jews because they serve God through their tradition. Not despite that but because of that! This is in sharp contrast to the language of "*Dominus Iesus*", where it is stated that only the Catholic Church has the full truth. This is no news, and to be fair, I suppose that a similar thesis, with an appropriate interpretation, would be proposed by every religion. But this shows how important the language used to express beliefs is, and how far reaching is "*Dabru emet*". In contrast to Ratzinger's document, which states that there are no parallel ways to redemption, here we read that there are equally valuable ways, one through the Torah and the Jewish tradition, another through Jesus and the tradition of the Church.

The natural question to ask is how many Jews share the attitude of the signers of "*Dabru emet*". It was written by four professors of Jewish studies, among them one woman, and has been coordinated by the Baltimore based Institute for Christian and Jewish Studies. The original 170 signatories were mostly Reform and Conservative Rabbis, with a handful of Orthodox, who have been active in Christian-Jewish dialogue. In October 2000, there were more than 200 signatories, including the present author.

The signatories are just a collection of individuals, even though the heads of some non-Orthodox rabbinical institutions are among them. Nothing significantly stronger may be expected. There exists no institution capable of speaking in the name of all Jews, or even of all religious Jews, or even of all Jews belonging to one stream of Judaism. Still, the over 200 individuals, who no doubt will be joined by more, are a significant group. In some non-Anglo-Saxon circles, notably in Israel and in Germany, attempts have been made to formulate similar declarations with more reference to local sensibilities. This is what the authors of "*Dabru emet*" hoped for. This is just the tip of the iceberg. Thousands of seriously committed Jews think similarly. We witnessed how "*Nostra Aetate*" both expressed and then shaped new attitudes; I believe that "*Dabru emet*" will help Jews to express positive opinions on Christianity and will influence the evolution of many others.

Rabbi Irving Greenberg has noted that as much as the evolution of the Church shows its strength, "ironically, this affirmation of Christianity shows that Judaism's vitality is undiminished; it too can self-correct."

4. Polish Accomplishments

Poland, the Polish Roman Catholic Church, and also Polish Jews, have taken part in the drama of the last decades. The unprecedented pastoral letter of the Polish Episcopate was issued on November 30, 1990, and was read in churches in January 1991. It contained for the first time an official presentation of the reorientation of the Catholic teaching on Jews and Judaism. It said that God has not taken his favour away from the Jewish people. Stressing the Jewish roots of the Church and the convergent messianic expectations gives a deep and strong basis to the condemnation of antisemitism. Moreover, the letter contains a discussion of issues from the recent history of Poland, including the Shoah and the post-war period.

The Polish Bishops questioned the self-righteous approach, common in Poland, concerning the attitudes to Jews during World War II. They wrote about irremovable "pangs of conscience", and asked for forgiveness. It was especially important that the Bishops told the Polish public that communists of Jewish origin had been motivated by communist ideology, and not by their ethnic background or (former) religion. In fact, that ideology required the same from *everyone*; to reject one's family traditions and, above all, religion. I would like to add that while the accusations against Jews for creating communism make no sense, it is, in my view, a moral challenge for Jews to take into account the fact that there were, relatively speaking, so many Jews among communists, and moreover, that some of them were involved in a fanatical, quasi-religious manner.[2]

Again, that document was important but to me it was not fully satisfying. The authors undermined their request for forgiveness by the statement that it would be necessary to ask for forgiveness even if there were "just one Christian" who could have helped but did not or acted against Jews. This suggests that only a few individuals behaved wrongly during World War II. But the fact is that indifference was very common, and anti-Jewish attitudes were not rare (see below). I believe that for Polish readers the phrase "just one" implies that the problem of Polish attitudes to Jews may be dismissed.

In some churches the letter was not read. This is by itself a proof its uniqueness. While the document inspired several positive reactions abroad, its impact in Poland has been limited. There have been few references to it. The majority seemed to forget about it rather quickly. Nevertheless, a breakthrough was made.

Nowadays some of the theses of the new teaching are well known. Although many Catholics ignore it, everybody has heard that antisemitism is a sin. The Polish Council of Christians and Jews published a booklet for teachers of religion, presenting the letter of the Polish Episcopate among excerpts of other documents introducing the new teachings. The Jewishness of Jesus is explained. This can be accepted by average parishioners, Father Michał Czajkowski likes to say, but the idea that Jesus' mother, St. Mary, the Queen of the Polish Crown, is Jewish, remains revolutionary.

There exists a permanent Committee of the Polish Episcopate devoted to the dialogue with Judaism. It organizes every year, on January 17, the Day of Judaism, which is a lesson of respect for the Jewish religion. Poland is the first country where this day has been

[2] See Chapter 4.

proclaimed as a national event.[3] The atmosphere has changed dramatically compared to the previous eras: it is normal to see interest in Judaism and Jewish culture among youth, also among Catholic seminary students. This does not necessarily go together with the readiness to admit guilt for attitudes and activities against Polish Jews. There are, however, events popularizing Jewish culture that seem to include a background message that Poland misses its Jews. Sometimes there is awareness that the story of the Shoah contains difficult challenges.

Another document, released on August 25, 2000, by the Polish Episcopal Council for Religious Dialogue, was approved by the Bishops' Conference. The result of long discussions and many drafts, the letter proclaims the need of an intricate "effort of the purification of memory." The longest section of the document is devoted to attitudes towards Jews. First, it reminds that the people of Israel have been chosen with an "irrevocable calling". Then it quotes a recent statement by Cardinal Józef Glemp, who asked forgiveness for "the attitudes of those who disregard people of other religions or tolerate antisemitism." After this, "sins from the time of the Shoah" are recalled, namely "indifference and enmity against Jews." Then the letter talks about the need to overcome anti-Jewish, anti-Judaic, and antisemitic attitudes. Finally, it says that anti-Polish and anti-Christian attitudes must be fought with similar determination.

The last point, comparing antisemitism to "antipolonism", was criticized by some Catholics, who say that regretting one's sins should not depend on the contrition of others; and by those who point out that there can be no comparison between the practical consequences of antisemitism and anti-Polish sentiment. To this Adam Michnik, the editor-in-chief of the most influential daily "*Gazeta Wyborcza*", himself of Jewish origin, replied that he agreed with the opinion that prejudices against Jews and against Poland are similarly abominable.

[3] More is said about the Day of Judaism in Poland in Chapter 8.

What is really new in the statement is the mention of "enmity". There is no example of hostile actions by Polish Christians against Jews, but what is said is an important step forward. It opens the way for consideration of those wartime events that are usually neglected.

Has there been an official reply by Polish Jews? Not yet. There was a general expression of satisfaction, but to produce an official statement is another matter: there is not enough experience in how to do that, and it would need to take into account the differences of opinion among Jews. At the same time, I am proud that the translation of "*Dabru emet*" into Polish was published in "*Gazeta Wyborcza*", the daily paper with the largest circulation, in September 2000, just three weeks after its publication.[4] This has been the first, and the only non-English language, version that reached masses of readers. While this is not to say that all the hundreds of thousands readers of the daily remember it, this does mean that in some respects Poland is among the leaders in Christian-Jewish dialogue.

5. Polish Challenges

For all the documents and achievements, Poland is at the beginning of a process. Is there less antisemitism in Poland today than in the past? No, many Polish Jews would say, as we hear time and again about Jews who are allegedly occupying the seats in the government, or the opponents' part of the soccer stadium. (Soccer fans use antisemitic slogans to insult the other team and its fans.) Moreover, the authors of many marginal publications write about "the Jewish danger" using language that has not changed since before World War II, as if there were still millions of Jews in Poland. The Shoah has had no perceptible impact on them. Also, express-

[4] *Gazeta Wyborcza* 30.09.2000. It also appeared in: *Studia Judaica* 3 (2000), *Więź* 8/2001, *Tygodnik Powszechny* 21/2001, *Studia i Dokumenty Ekumeniczne* Nr 1/2001, *Znak* 1/2003, and other periodicals.

ing antisemitism is socially acceptable too often in today's Poland. Still, the fact is that it is much harder now than ever before to affirm both Christianity and antisemitism. But there is a long way to go. A small but instructive example is given by the case of a picture in the Sandomierz cathedral.

The seventeenth-century picture shows the alleged ritual murder by Jews of a Christian child in the city. It is worse than mere untruth. It is a representation of the motif that served as a pretext for anti-Jewish violence. The accusation of alleged murder by Jews led to actual murder of Jews. The local Church has not responded to numerous requests to remove the picture. Some defenders of the present situation argue on aesthetic grounds that the interior of the church would be ruined if the picture disappears. This I can understand. The local Church authorities are, however, similarly unresponsive to moderate proposals; the Polish Council of Christians and Jews offered to finance a plaque with explanations of the blood libel and information about the official statements by various Popes rejecting the accusation. The issue has recently become well known. Israeli tour groups come to see this example of antisemitism, and Polish critics, including priests like Father Stanisław Musiał, say that the picture is good only for a museum of antisemitism. The locals resent the outside intervention, and some guides suggest that the events did happen, because "a Jewish sect" practiced ritual murder. The silence of the local Bishop shows that the task of "the purification of memory" is difficult even in seemingly simple cases. The Polish Council of Christians and Jews[5] has also tried to intervene. The text of a plaque was devised, explaining that the blood libel is not only false but was described by the popes as such. No progress whatsoever has been made so far, despite promises by various authorities.

We are in a special situation conducting Christian-Jewish dialogue in Poland. It is the place of the Shoah. Although Poles refuse

[5] See Chapter 8 for some information.

to accept this, I suppose that the best-known place-name in Poland is Auschwitz. This is the cause of difficulties, as well as of the special importance of our dialogue. It may require courage, as suggested by the Polish Episcopal letter of August 2000.

In the 1998 Vatican document "*We remember*" we read that the authors "deeply regret the errors and failures of those sons and daughters of the Church" who failed. How? "We cannot know how many Christians in countries occupied or ruled by the Nazi powers or their allies were horrified at the disappearance of their Jewish neighbours and yet were not strong enough to raise their voices in protest." Horrified – but not strong enough. Were it only that! This sounds like a joke. This is not the source of Jewish psychological wounds. Jews remember indifference, enmity (mentioned in the letter of the Polish Church), and satisfaction; the only thing Hitler did well, one could hear, was that he solved the Jewish problem. Many people still remember covert or overt satisfaction that Jews had disappeared and it was possible to take over their houses. How many thousands of houses and possessions were taken over by neighbours? We do not really know as no historians estimated the extent of the ownership changes. We also do not know the scope of post-war hostility towards the survivors when they returned to their towns. Many of them had to escape. Some were murdered. Average Poles know next to nothing about those facts. And we do not know "how many Christians" were guilty of the anti-Jewish attitudes. It is important to overcome the taboo about those facts if the process of teshuvah and reconciliation is to continue.

And the post-war attitudes are not the most difficult challenge. The most difficult part is that the Shoah was not only witnessed by Polish Christians, not only that some of them benefited, but that in some cases they took part in murder.

The Jedwabne story is well known by now, due to the book *Neighbours*, by Jan Gross. It appeared in 2000, and was preceded by work done on a TV documentary film by Agnieszka Arnold from Warsaw. Actually, since then, the book has been superseded by two major publications: two volumes of documents and analysis published in by the National Remembrance Institute[6] and the recent book by Anna Bikont[7]. The story is about one day in July 1941, a few weeks after German conquered the territories in Eastern Poland that had been occupied by the Soviets since 1939. In Jedwabne, a small town, on July 10, hundreds of Jews[8], or nearly all who lived there, were killed by their neighbours. The Germans were in control of the area but did not participate. This event has become widely known only recently. The matter had never been discussed in Poland, so it had not entered the picture of Polish history. No signs of shame, repentance, or moral reflection were seen for almost 60 years. Only recently initiatives appeared to recognize the tragedy, and to pay homage to the victims. Murder in Jedwabne is even more horrible than the Kielce pogrom of 1946. In 2001, during the sixtieth anniversary of the massacre, President Aleksander Kwaśniewski, in a remarkable speech, apologized in the name of "all those who felt there was a reason to apologize". The resulting moral challenge has yet to be met on the local level. Most people in the town reject the challenge, and agree with the position of the recently departed parish priest and the local bishop who presented the affair as a "Jewish attack" against Poland. The most shocking example of the negative attitudes is provided by the story of Antonina Wyrzykowska, a woman who hid a group of Jews after the massacre. The Jews survived the war, yet she was not seen as hero by her neighbours but rather as someone who could discredit the others, and under pressure she had to move, eventually going to America.

[6] Paweł Machcewicz, Krzysztof Persak (eds.) *Wokół Jedwabnego*, IPN, Warszawa 2002.

[7] Anna Bikont, *My z Jedwabnego*, Prószyński i S-ka, Warszawa 2004.

[8] I originally wrote 1600, after Jan Gross' *Neighbours*; he took it from the memorial erected there in 1970s. After the research done by the Institute of National Remembrance, it seems that the number was smaller, but nobody knows the exact number of the victims.

It is extremely difficult for anyone, anywhere to confront shameful events of one's history. The role of the Church can be crucial. If young people were able to handle the burden of the past, it would mean that the difficult process of the teshuvah of the Church would have borne fruit. What has been done by the Church seems less than adequate. No official Church representative took part in the Jedwabne commemoration in 2001. However, two weeks earlier the bishops organized an unprecedented penitential service in a Warsaw church. One prayer read, "Let us pray … for all who harbour ill will and resentment towards the Jewish nation that they may accept from God the grace of a change of heart." Many bishops knelt down in repentance. In this way they accepted moral responsibility. The powerful gesture had no perceptible consequence. Neither the local bishop nor the parishioners in Jedwabne changed their minds. What is more, the church in which the service was held has a bookshop in the basement, stocking a full range of the standard antisemitic literature on sale in Poland. And the bookshop is still there in 2005. Therefore it is hard not to ask how sincere the gesture was.

I am not trying to suggest that it is only the Church who needs repentance. This task applies to all of us as individuals; we all need to overcome resentments and hatred. Also, other communities should be involved in the process of teshuvah. For example, the ancient conquest of Canaan remains a difficulty, and the military rule over Arabs in recent decades continues to be a source of moral challenge. Obviously, the Jewish community is not burdened by anything comparable to the Shoah. Yet, according to Rabbi Irving Greenberg,

Ultimately, the touchstone of Judaism's integrity in response to the Holocaust is whether it can purge itself of attitudes that promulgate hatred and whether it can neutralize classic texts that may generate contempt for others.

One wonders which is harder: to make a teshuvah or to sincerely accept someone else's teshuvah?

Catholic-jewish Dialogue In Post-war Poland

Note

The paper partly overlaps with other similar papers: one prepared for a lecture in June 1997 at the Oxford Centre for Hebrew and Jewish Studies, and another for a conference organized in March 1998 by the Center for the Study of Human Rights of Columbia University in Krakow. A portion of the text is adapted from a chapter of my (Polish) book *Żydzi, judaizm, Polska (Jews, Judaism, Poland)*. The update contains only a fraction of the factual data that could have been included. But if done the chapter would become a chronicle of events rather than a reflection on problems.

My topic is dialogue and since there is no such thing as an abstract dialogue – because specific conditions and experiences of the dialogue participants constitute essential ingredients of the dialogue relationship – let me remind the reader that I write as a *Polish* Polish Jew, one of those who live in Poland and treat Poland as their space and not just a place of origin. *Our* space – and when I say "our" I mean belonging, familiarity, connection, value, and meaning.

1. Christian-Jewish versus Polish-Jewish Dialogue

Speaking about the Christian-Jewish dialogue in Poland people often use the term "Polish-Jewish" dialogue. This is understandable from a foreign perspective. For an English Jew, even if he is of Polish origin, basically Poles are Christian, which would mean that Jews are not Poles. This *façon de parler* was also common in pre-war Poland, when Polonized Jews were a minority among Jews, and only minorities on both sides accepted the idea that one can be both Jewish and Polish. This has gradually changed after the war, and now – let me repeat – most of us *are* Polish.

Interestingly enough, new language has not been introduced, and often the terminology "Poles and Jews" is still used in Poland. I find it mistaken. The fact is, however, that the phrase "Christians and Jews" that I prefer to use is not perfect either. It leaves out those Poles who are not really Christian and who are not Jewish. How serious is it? Perhaps not too much: going back one or two generations we almost always have clear group belonging, so virtually everyone is "Jewish by origin" or "Christian by origin".

Two problems arise here: first, the matter of mixed origins, second, the problem of the nature of the Jewish community.

Many of us are of mixed parentage. This has implications for our identities - which is a complex topic discussed at length by many authors (and ordinary Jews too). It is clear that the co-existence of Jewish and non-Jewish Polish roots in one person makes one even more a *Polish* Polish Jew. There exists also a very important consequence of this situation for the Christian-Jewish dialogue proper. I believe that the Christian-Jewish dialogue can be properly conducted only by people with strong, secure identities. It is not a place for identity seekers. Or rather, while the seekers can be extremely valuable in dialogue, they cannot be the main actors; there would be too much confusion otherwise.

The second problem can be reduced to the question: What sort of a minority are we? I believe that we, as Jews, are members of a religious minority. Yet I know that many disagree, and what is more important, it is not really possible to differentiate between Judaism as a religion and Jewishness, meaning belonging to the Jewish people. Those two dimensions, as well as cultural and tribal ones, are intermingled. As a matter of fact, no single general category seems to fit the phenomenon of Jewishness. Yet to anti-religious Jews, Jewishness is either irrelevant or purely national. From their perspective being Polish and Jewish at the same time may seem impossible. Then the dialogue can be only Polish-Jewish.

To me it is Polish-Polish, that is, the dialogue in Poland constitutes a Polish section of the universal Christian-Jewish dialogue. I believe this approach will be more and more accepted, especially as Poland is integrated into Western structures.

2. The meaning of "dialogue"

Dialogue in a weak sense means that there are contacts, so that people are not isolated from each other but rather engage in conversation and exchange. In this sense dialogue is of course common, and in fact it is so obvious in contemporary Poland that nobody can even imagine its absence. I remember my surprise when Rafael ("Felek") Scharf, the unforgettable Krakow-born friend from London, who finished university in pre-war Krakow, explained that during his youth in Poland he never paid a visit to a non-Jewish home. In the 1990s, when he came to his native city from London, where he had been living since 1939, he was often a guest in homes of the most famous Polish writers, and this was perfectly natural for everyone. This shows well the new reality, the reality which we all take for granted.

The new reality for me, and even more for those younger than me, means that we Jews and our Christian peers share most life experiences: educational, political, and cultural. For example, my generation has been marked by a participation in the initial "Solidarity" movement in the 1980s, where all could participate equally. Only in specifically Jewish contexts did our Jewishness become relevant.[1]

Thus when I speak about dialogue, I mean primarily an exchange between Jews *as Jews* and Christians *as Christians*. Part of the dialogue, albeit in a very shallow meaning of the term, takes place in the framework of political contacts. Meetings of official representatives, mutual participation at commemorations, discussions concerning the restitution of Jewish communal property, etc. are important. Occasionally they are even vital. Yet the political game, important as it is, cannot be called dialogue in any deeper sense. It only provides a part of the background.

Dialogue in a strong sense must touch deeper; the specific experiences of each side must be shared and heard with respect. In the Polish situation, specifically Christian experiences are mostly familiar to Jews. The opposite is not true: a special interest and goodwill is necessary if Christians want to understand the specific experiences of Jews in Poland.

Ultimately Christian-Jewish dialogue should refer to a deeper bond between the two sides: at stake is a theological brotherhood. Perhaps its most important proponent was Franz Rosenzweig, to whom I feel a special spiritual affinity. He presented a vision in which both Judaism and Christianity are indispensable – each in its own way – for God's relationship with (hu)mankind. When the vision of brotherhood is shared despite the legacy of conflict then the participants in dialogue can do more than negotiate, discuss or exchange experiences; they can support each other in the difficult task of promoting deeper dialogue in their own religious communities.

In connection with this let me mention a very interesting example. Among the first thinkers who introduced Rosenzweig to Polish intellectual public was the philosopher Father Józef Tischner

[1] For an account written from the perspective of that time see Chapter 5.

of Krakow. Very active in Polish public life, he first became popular in 1981 when he became an unofficial chaplain of "Solidarity", that initial romantic "Solidarity" that included all opponents of communism. Tischner and his students were also very active in introducing Emmanuel Lévinas and the philosophy of dialogue. At the same time, Father Tischner had an ambition to create a Polish philosophy, expressing the experiences of Poles and the miracle of "Solidarity", where then there was space for us all, and which feels so distant from today's narrowly political, heavily Christian trade union of the same name. Back then I felt optimistic; the intellectual mentor of a 10 million-member movement was also an interpreter of contemporary philosophers, who represented the highest achievement of Jewish thought in this century. Unfortunately a lot has changed; until his recent death Father Tischner continued his penetrating thinking and friendship with some liberal thinkers, like the famous former dissident Adam Michnik, but gradually he became marginalized in the Polish Church. Many fundamentalist traditionalists, including some leaders of the present-day "Solidarity", treat him as a traitor, alien to genuine Polish Catholic thinking.

While Father Tischner was not directly involved in Christian-Jewish dialogue, his story illustrates several aspects of our situation, namely, the close personal ties of individual Christians and Jews, the evolution of "Solidarity", and tensions within the Catholic Church.

3. Early post-war decades: no dialogue in Poland

In general, Christian-Jewish dialogue nowhere began before World War II. The shock of the Shoah, and then the establishment of the state of Israel, led to a deeper dialogue in the West.

In Poland, the shock was almost nonexistent, and certainly it was not expressed. This was probably due to the fact that the general Polish suffering was so acute. Also, paradoxically the closeness of the death camps made reflection harder; for many years, accounts of events dominated, and reflection on their historic significance came later.

In immediate post-war years official Christian-Jewish encounters were dominated by problems related to anti-Jewish violence, the most famous being the Kielce pogrom of 1946, in which 42 Jews were killed. It began with rumours of the disappearance of a Polish child and the repetition of the age-old accusation that Jews used the blood of Christian children in their rituals, the "blood libel". Jews tried to get from the bishops a statement condemning the blood libel; with the exception of Bishop Tadeusz Kubina of Częstochowa, who officially proclaimed that "all allegations about ritual murder were false", they were unsuccessful. The bishops felt that Jews were too influential among the cadres of the new regime, and anti-Jewish attitudes came as a reaction to that. All those contacts prompted by pogroms belong to the pre-history of the Polish dialogue but they did not constitute any particular achievement.

It is essential to remember that under Stalinism dialogue was difficult in any area. Dialogue requires a minimum of security and freedom. The Church was under attack, and was preoccupied with the fight for survival. There were few Polish Jews. Those who cared about their Jewishness were even fewer in number, and were also preoccupied with the fight for survival, that is, survival as Jews. Jewish institutions after about 1950 were completely dominated by communists who did not even think about treating religious Christians seriously.[2] There was almost nobody who both felt a connection to the tradition and had enough openness with respect to the Church to try to make deeper contact. And anyway, Poland, being overwhelmingly Catholic, could enter official dialogue with Jews only after the Second Vatican Council.

Having said all this, I still do not understand why there was no attempt at dialogue among intellectuals. Individuals occasionally

[2] More information can be found in Chapter 6.

did things despite the system, even under Stalinist terror. Christian-Jewish contacts were numerous but the discussion and the intellectual arguments, which often degenerated into political ones, did not include problems that are associated with Christian-Jewish dialogue. Probably, the lack of Jews was one of the main reasons; that is, of committed and open-minded Jews, who would like to affirm Judaism and at the same time feel to be equal partners with Christian intellectuals. Jewish intellectuals were distancing themselves from Judaism. As I was once told by an outstanding Polish writer, Julian Stryjkowski, who came from a traditional Jewish milieu, and wrote mostly about Jews, "Jewishness was only a misfortune"; Polon ization meant abandonment of Jewish commitment.

It was not until some time after the Second Vatican Council, and after the 1967 Six-Day war, and also after the forced emigration of some 15,000 Polish Jews in 1968 and 1969, that Polish Catholic intellectuals began the work of establishing the early stages of dialogue in Poland. Learning about Judaism became as important as condemning antisemitism. To my knowledge, there were two notable dialogue achievements in the 1970s and early 1980s. The first included publications of liberal Catholic monthlies: *Znak*, much of the time edited by Stefan Wilkanowicz, *Więź*, and the weekly *Tygodnik Powszechny*, under the leadership of Jerzy Turowicz. The second achievement was the annual "Jewish Culture Week", organized by the Catholic Intellectuals' Club, or KIK, in Warsaw, and specifically by Krzysztof Śliwiński.[3] Young people, not only Catholics, first came together to clean the Jewish cemetery in Warsaw, and then met with Jewish authors, and experts on Jewish culture. I remember in particular meetings with Marek Edelman, a former leader of the Warsaw ghetto uprising[4], with the historian Szymon Datner, and

[3] In free Poland, Śliwiński served as the first Polish Ambassador for Contacts with the Jewish Diaspora, and recently was the ambassador to South Africa.

[4] More about his role in the Solidarity period is contained in Chapter 5.

the writer Julian Stryjkowski. Many of those people, both Catholics and Jews, had participated together in cultural occasions or worked in connection with political, that is dissident, activities. Here for the first time they were meeting in a systematic, friendly way to share, Jews *as Jews* and Christians *as Christians*. The contacts and friendships made then were helpful in dialogue later.

Since the 1980s, important contributions have been made by historians from Poland and other countries who, starting with a conference in Oxford in 1984, began serious collaboration on the history of Jews in Poland. Historical research on Jewish-related questions has advanced very considerably in the past two decades. More generally, the free market and the absence of censorship have led to an explosion of books on Jewish subjects: on both the history of the Jews and Judaism. Many of these books are translated from other languages, but there have been some valuable original Polish works. Some themes are covered better in Poland than anywhere else in the world. This is true of Polish editions of the wartime memoirs of Polish Jews and of studies of the Kielce pogrom. Some other sensitive topics are now studied in more details in Poland than elsewhere. For example, books appeared in 2004 about the blackmail of Jews in hiding in German-occupied Poland, and about reporting to Gestapo by seemingly average citizens, also during World War II.[5]

Historical research, important as it is, does not constitute the core of the religious based dialogue we talk about. The real history of this dialogue in Poland, as opposed to pre-history, began in 1986. Let me illustrate the interest in dialogue with figures.

The book, *Bibliography of Christian-Jewish Dialogue in Poland in 1945-1995* by Miroslaw Mikolajczyk, lists 2,593 items – books and articles related to the dialogue (but not those only on Jewish history or on Judaism), published in Polish. While the list contains some

5 Jan Grabowski *Ja tego Żyda znam! Szantażowanie Żydów w Warszawie 1939-1943*, Wydawnictwo IFiS PAN, Warszawa 2004, and Barbara Engleking-Boni *Szanowny panie Gistapo*, Wydawnictwo IFiS PAN, Warszawa 2004.

pieces written with more or less antisemitic bias, a considerable majority is written in a spirit of sympathy, which is to me an indispensable part of real dialogue (required, of course, on each side). Only relatively important texts are included. The numbers corresponding to each year are revealing. In the years 1945-1949 there were 42 items. Between 1950 and 1956 – none! In general, in the 1950s – 29 items; in the 1960s – 182 items; in the 1970s – 160 items; in the 1980s – 833 items (of which 622 items belong to the period 1986-1990); and from 1991 to 1995 – 1347 items. From 1996 to 2000 there were, I have been told by the bibliographer, 2416 items! Later the exponential growth seems to have continued.

In the area of dialogue, as much as in many other areas, the new Poland has developed in 1980s and underwent an explosive growth in 1990s. In the recent years the dialogue has grown further, which is not to say that attitudes hostile to dialogue have disappeared.

4. Historical background issues specific to the dialogue in Poland

Christian-Jewish dialogue in Poland involves all the general themes – the Christian theological reorientation, antisemitism, the bond between Christians and Jews – but naturally the stress is on the past. To overcome the burden of the past is an important part of the dialogue anywhere. In Poland the tragic past is more tangible, and more controversial than in many other countries, as there are several events and phenomena in recent history that influence our dialogue.

4.1. The Thesis Pole = Catholic

The association of Catholicism with being Polish, rooted in the nineteenth century when Poland was partitioned mainly by Orthodox Russia and Protestant Prussia, still remains widespread. Not often expressed directly, it is seen as obvious by a good number of Poles, including many Church leaders for whom the only natural

Polish existence is to be an active member of the Catholic Church. Under such an approach all non-Catholics are threatened with marginalization. And, obviously, Jews have been the prime example of non-Catholics in Poland.

Curiously, in post-war Poland Jews who have become Catholics can also meet with suspicion. The "Pole = Catholic" thesis has been interpreted to mean that a real Pole means someone whose family has been Catholic for generations. (This often leads to a search for "disguised" Jews.)

It seems, however, that with Poland being a member of the European Union this attitude is diminishing, especially among younger and better educated Poles.

4.2. Suffering in the Polish Tradition

In the background of our Polish dialogue there is the Polish Romantic tradition that includes a specific Messianism. According to this view, Poles are the chosen nation, and suffer as "the Christ of the nations". This image, created by nineteenth-century poets, is completely unknown outside Poland. It is still important, although the last few years have witnessed the rise of pragmatic attitudes distant from Romantic categories of thought. Yet those categories are at the root of a specific Polish phenomenon – competition in suffering with the Jews.

Who suffered more during World War II? Many Poles feel that Poles suffered at least as much as Jews. While this contradicts the global image of that period it reflects the fact that the cruelty of the German occupation in Poland was directed against everyone. Virtually every Polish family lost some members. Ninety percent of Polish Jews, however, were murdered. It is probably possible for Poles to ignore the difference only because of the Polish self-image of Poles as victims *par excellence*.

The result is that it is usually not understood in Poland that the Shoah constitutes a challenge to Christianity. The realization that the mass murder of Jews occurred in the middle of Christian

Europe is among the main points of reflection for Christians in the Christian-Jewish dialogue. Few Poles feel it; most say that Germans were guilty, not Christians. Thinking about World War II, Poles see rather a bond of common suffering with Jews than the bond of common Christianity with Germans.[6]

4.3. Post-war Antisemitism

The Kielce pogrom of July 1946, in which 42 Jews were killed by a mob, is a symbol of a tragic legacy that is not easy to discuss. The moral responsibility is recognized by some Poles but most try to blame others, for example Soviet agents, as the only people guilty of that crime, so that Poles emerge innocent. Only relatively few Poles, such as Jan Błoński in his important article in a Catholic intellectual weekly,[7] recognize the moral challenge publicly. As usual, there is a paradox; those who feel moral responsibility the most are those who are actually least responsible. I might add parenthetically that the studies by historians and the official investigation by the public prosecutor, which ended in 1997, brought no breakthroughs in regard to the "provocation theory" that was supposed to explain the pogrom. Such a provocation cannot be ruled out, but there is no evidence for any of the versions that have been advanced. The most important fact remains the susceptibility of Poles (some Poles, of course) to a deadly form of antisemitic hysteria at that time.

The years immediately after the war gave rise to divergent experiences. Let me illustrate one point mentioning again Father Tischner, whom I respected very deeply. He came from the Tatra mountain region. He remembered from his childhood the activities of highlander partisans ("Ogień" group) just after the war, and associated them with the battle for freedom and independence, with something

6 On related issues connected to Auschwitz, see Chapter 1.

7 Jan Blonski, "The Poor Poles Look at the Ghetto", Four Decades of Polish Essays, ed. Jan Kott. Northwestern UP, 1990, pp. 222-235, originally published in *Tygodnik Powszechny* 2/1987.

genuine and positive, despite possible abuses committed by them.[8] To me, the main association is different; those partisans murdered some Jews who happened to be in the area. It is hard, if at all possible, to overcome these disparate memories. At the same time I find it at least as significant that we have so much is common; from the love of the Tatra Mountains to the original "Solidarity" movement to the philosophy of Emmanuel Lévinas.

The antisemitic propaganda of 1968, the resulting purges, and finally the emigration of a majority of Polish Jews, many deeply Polonized, were without parallel in post-war Europe. Direct responsibility belongs to the ruling communists but the significance of that antisemitic, anti-liberal and anti-intellectual campaign can be seen – to use the phrase of Adam Michnik – in the attempt to adapt Polish extreme right-wing traditions for use by the Communist Party. It is hard to say how much popular support was generated by that antisemitic campaign. There was no free expression of opinion. Individual experiences range from hostility to solidarity. Judging from the experience of free Poland of 1990s where antisemitic attitudes are quite widespread, it is possible to guess that there was some general support to the purges.

I must stress, however, that despite antisemitism, the events of 1968 – the student revolt, the demand for freedom – produced common experiences between people like me and the Catholic intelligentsia, which were also attacked. Many of our experiences were the same. We were on the same side of the barricade then, and very often later in the dissident movement of the 1970s and 1980s. Today, this is helpful as we deepen our dialogue.

4.4. Jewish Communists

Time and again, in meetings with Polish Catholics, I meet with outbursts of resentment against Jewish communists or Jews as com-

[8] Józef Tischner, "Sprawa Józefa Kurasia 'Ognia'," *Tygodnik Powszechny*, September 1, 1996.

munists. This has become most obvious in the debate around the 1941 Jedwabne massacre. Yet even in the context of a nominally religious dialogue suddenly there are people who want to talk about "*Żydzi w UB*" or Jews in the Stalinist secret service. Of course, it is an expression of antisemitism, but it would be wrong to simply dismiss the problem behind it. And the fact is that there were very many visible, prominent Jews in the early period of communist Poland. The sheer number of those Jewish communists participating in the system of terror, and their fanaticism, does pose a problem for us Jews. Of course, I am not proposing blaming only the Jews and absolving others (as my critics sometimes suggest).

I only want to stress three points, all explained in Chapter 4 of this book. The first two are simply facts, the third is an interpretation. First, communism, broadly understood, belongs also to Jewish history, and not just to the history of Poland, Russia, or Europe. Second, in post-war Poland, and more generally in the middle of the twentieth century in Europe, Jews were not only among the victims of oppression (which, of course, is the dominant part of the picture) but also among the oppressors. The third, and more controversial, claim is that Jews in Poland or elsewhere have (too rarely, I believe) dared to take up the resulting moral challenge. I believe this can be made part of the dialogue agenda, provided that good will can be assumed on both sides. I think that it would be wrong to leave the topic of Jewish communists to antisemites.

4.5. Denying the Existence of Antisemitism

A common denominator of many troublesome elements in Polish attitudes to Jews can be seen in the denial of the existence of antisemitism. It is amazing that even Father Jankowski of Gdansk claimed that he was no antisemite, shortly after making a sermon to the effect that the Star of David is the sinister symbol of the threats to Poland. He probably wanted to say that he was not guilty of saying something wrong, but rather the Jews were guilty, which is a classic antisemitic motif. Recently, he sued Paweł Huelle, a writer from Gdansk, who had reproached him for holding Nazi-like views.

Part of the reason for dismissing the existence of antisemitic attitudes probably comes from Polish history. If we understand antisemitism as murder – let alone when we subconsciously see it as *mass* murder! – then mere words of hate are seen as insignificant. We need to remind ourselves that poisoned words can lead to criminal actions. Dialogue can be helpful here.

Antisemitism in today's Poland is often completely abstract. It is not so much that Jews are blamed as enemies but that enemies are labelled as Jewish. This is most striking in the case of football fans who taunt the other team and its fans with the chant: "Jews to the gas!" On the other hand, antisemitism in Poland is always expressed in the same way: there are too many Jews. There are people who still say this. The truth is that there are very few affiliated Jews and almost all of those who occupy important positions have nothing to do with Jewish life. Most of them would not even admit that they are of Jewish origin.[9]

Many Jews are still hiding their origins. I find this sad. To overcome antisemitism would mean to have the situation in which it would seem natural that there can be a Jew in the government who on Jewish holidays participates in synagogue celebrations. We are far from this level. I feel, however, that a slow development towards less hostile attitudes, and less inhibition among Jews, is taking place in Poland. It was seen at a session on the thirtieth anniversary of the events of March 1968 that I helped organize in Warsaw. Czeslaw Bielecki, the man who was later the chairman of the Foreign Relations Committee of the Polish parliament, whose parents had left then for Israel in 1968, stated in public: "I have worked all

[9] A description of the situation is contained in Chapter 6.

my life to make antisemites afraid of me." This says something important about him, and about present day Poland.

5. The Polish Catholic Church

In Poland today, Roman Catholics constitute 90% of the population. The Polish Catholic Church is the main force in the Christian-Jewish dialogue in Poland. That is why the developments within the Church are important for our topic.

5.1. The Pope and the Parishioners

In Poland, as much as in Western countries, dialogue takes place against the background of the post-Vatican II openness of segments of the Catholic Church to Jewish traditions. In Catholic revivalist movements like "Neokatechumenat" or youth groups like "Oazy" Hebrew songs are sung, Judaism is seen as a valuable point of reference. One of the major goals of "Neokatechumenat" is to regain the Jewish roots of the church. Most Jews in Poland are happy to witness the Christian search for Jewish roots, and some try to help in it.

John Paul II made major contributions to Christian-Jewish dialogue. As we all remember, he developed further the reorientation of the teaching about Jews adopted at the Second Vatican Council, he called antisemitism a sin, visited the synagogue in Rome, and established full diplomatic relations with the state of Israel, where he visited both the Western ("Wailing") Wall and Yad Vashem.[10] He was a Pole, and his Polish experiences helped him to have a deeper approach to the question of the Church's relations with Jews. He had personal contacts with Jews in Krakow (he used to visit the president of the Jewish community at home), he had witnessed the murder of Jews during the war. (I think that he was the first pope

[10] In Chapter 7, I give a few more details concerning the Church new teachings and how they developed.

in centuries who saw Jews not as abstract figures only but real life neighbours.) His close contacts and friendships with Jews, most notably with his schoolmate Jerzy Kluger, were recalled in Poland immediately after his death. The Polish background of his teachings is actually deeper than foreigners realize. The famous saying about Jews being elder brothers in faith was taken – as I have already mentioned in Chapter 7 – from the Polish Romantic poet Mickiewicz, who had used it in a pro-Jewish way. That is why it is certain that the pope used it respectfully and was certainly not trying to suggest the replacement thesis, the anti-Jewish thesis which naturally comes to mind for those whose only association with the metaphor are the Biblical examples: the younger brother replacing the older in the intimate relationship to God.

It is only in some less visible areas that I find his approach hard to accept. For example, he repeatedly said that the tragedy of the Shoah was "our common tragedy" and that it was so great that it must eventually bear fruit. Whatever might be meant by bearing fruit, I believe it is too easy a jump from death to resurrection. This can be described as "too Christian", although it is true that some Jews say much the same thing proposing their favourite kinds of fruit (from the creation of the state of Israel to the prospect of complete Orthodoxy for all). And, actually, even those words of the Pope can be understood as an appeal to constructive effort, to build despite the tragedy.

Whatever criticism we can make of the Pope's words, his message to the Poles was consistent and clear: respect the Jews and their religion. This has influenced Poles. According to a survey[11] after (and relating to) the visit of John Paul II to Israel, 55% of Poles said that when the Pope apologized for the wrongs done to Jews, he said just the right thing. Also, in the previous four years there was a significant increase of the Poles who see the common religious roots of

[11] A survey by one of the major agencies, CBOS, in the year 2000.

Christians and Jews – about one half thought so in 2000, including the "elder brethren" clause; and the more religious Catholics are, the more are they ready to accept that. About one half of Poles seemed to be ready to work on the improvement of relations with Jews. John Paul II is a hero in Poland, genuinely respected and indeed revered more than anyone before. This makes life hard for all those who combine Christianity with explicit antisemitism. This combination was common before the war and has not disappeared. The difference is that now they either oppose the teaching of the late Pope, which is very rare in Poland, or have to find indirect terms, and include Jews in larger categories like Freemasons, Trotskyites, "Europeans", etc. Even though the blend of Catholic and antisemitic views persists, it is hard to say that it is a majority view, and it is much harder than before to present it as the official Church approach.

Opinion polls seemed to show that the religiously motivated antisemitism decreased in 1990s, and what remained was primarily political antisemitism, directed more against assimilated Jews than against Judaism. In fact, the most virulent antisemitic words and activities come from extremists like skinheads and similar groups who are either openly anti-Catholic, or at least say that the Vatican has been under a pernicious Jewish influence. Yet more recent surveys[12] suggest that strongly "modern antisemitic" attitudes (not religiously based but rather referring to power, influence, subversion) grew (from 17% in 1992 to 27% in 2002), and "traditional antisemitism" (Jews as Christ-killers etc.) has remained the same (at 11%). At the same time, opposition to antisemitism has grown (classified as strong from 8% to 16%, and milder one from 13% to 19%). The results confirm my general feeling that we have been witnessing a polarization in Poland: more antisemitic attitudes and more opposition to them. It seems to be related to a growing self-

[12] Reported in the book "Anti-Semitism in Poland and in Ukraine" by Ireneusz Krzemiński and others (Scholar, Warsaw 2004).

confidence, itself a result of the awareness that the Polish nation has become a legitimate member of the family of the developed nations. Thus people are more ready to express opinions that in the immediately post-communist years.

Sometimes the fact that both Jews and Christians can be seen as targets finds concrete expression. On February 26, 1997, the Warsaw synagogue was set on fire. Fortunately, firemen came immediately and only the entrance and vestibule were damaged. Until today nothing is known about the arsonist. The way it was done suggested a carefully prepared act. The incident was perceived as a serious sign of antisemitism. Paradoxically, it gave an occasion to an unprecedented expression of solidarity with Jews. High ranking politicians and leaders of churches, including the head of the Polish president's office, the deputy speakers of the House and the Senate, were present in the synagogue at the service next day. Some who were not present or properly represented, for example the Catholic bishops, issued statements with words of solidarity. Whatever the motivations, the message was clear; antisemitic acts were not to be tolerated by Polish elite.

A month later, a sixteenth-century wooden church in Katowice was set on fire. One wall was burned. St. Michael's church had been set on fire four times since 1995. In June 1997, the police caught suspected arsonists, a group of skinheads. The press reported it but it was an incomparably smaller piece of news in Poland than the synagogue fire, and of course outside Poland it aroused no interest at all. Not surprisingly, the parish priest was angry; "where is the president," he complained, "who immediately came to the synagogue?"

One can give reasons why the fire in the only synagogue in Warsaw is symbolically more powerful than fire in one of thousands of Polish churches; but the fact remains that extremists can be similarly harmful to both, and that they can come from families living in the neighbourhood. Similarly, desecration of cemeteries happens at all kinds of cemeteries, so by itself it does not distinguish Jewish cemeteries from Christian ones. Of course, sometimes desecration of Jewish cemeteries is motivated by antisemitism. It is, however, a mistake to assume that it must be so. Vandals who enjoy destruction attack Christian cemeteries even more often than the Jewish ones. Satanists, who enjoy desecration of symbols holy to the dominant religions, destroy graves at Catholic cemeteries. Of course, I am not trying to justify desecration. I am only saying that so often our understanding of the significance of specific event from distant places has more to do with our global image of the place than with the details of the events. And the image is often based on prejudice.

5.2. The Divided Church

In recent years, divisions in the Polish Catholic church, and indeed within the Episcopate, have been presented openly to the public for the first time in many generations. The first occasion was provided by the debate before the national referendum that was supposed to approve (or reject) the new constitution. It was approved by a small majority in May 1997, but only 42% turned out to vote. The final text resulted from a compromise of major parties and the church. It was engineered by Tadeusz Mazowiecki, a well-known politician; the first non-communist prime Minister in 1989 and a noted Catholic intellectual, who had consulted on the text with Bishop Tadeusz Pieronek, then the secretary of the Episcopate. He approved the words with which God was mentioned in the preamble ("We, the Polish Nation – all citizens of the Republic, both those who believe in God as the source of truth, justice, good, and beauty, as well as those not sharing such faith but respecting those universal values as arising from other sources"[13]) and the way the protection of human life was formulated ("The Republic of Po-

[13] *The Constitution of the Republic of Poland*, (trans. Albert Pol), Sejm Publishing Office, Warsaw 1999, p.3.

land shall ensure the legal protection of the life of every human being"[14]). Pieronek remained loyal and repeated all the time that a reasonable compromise had been achieved, and that the Church would not say how individuals should vote. Other bishops, however, prevailed and issued an official statement saying that everyone was free to vote as they wished but morality is all-important and the proposed text was morally flawed. Some bishops went much further, claiming that the constitution promoted a New Age concept of God, and was directed against human life and against Polish sovereignty. A massive and virulent campaign was organized by the right wing and the church. The atmosphere has been aptly characterized by Aleksander Smolar. According to him, the strife was seen by the Conservatives as a conflict of two civilizations; "Christian-national-patriotic Poland defends Faith, Fatherland and Family against liberal-communist-Masonic-Jewish-relativistic-postmodern attack." While that specific issue is almost forgotten in everyday political debates, a similar front has recently been opened in connection with the arguments concerning the European Constitution.

Incidentally, Smolar is the director of the Polish Soros Foundation, called the Stefan Batory Foundation, which has greatly supported education for democracy and has helped innumerable cultural and scholarly activities in recent years. The foundation, and George Soros himself, have been virulently attacked by the conservative right wing as the stronghold of Masonic conspiracy that wants to kill Christianity and morality, and eventually rule the world.

Perhaps the most influential in the attacks against liberalism is the network of radio stations, "Radio Maryja". The radio, presenting itself as "the Catholic voice in your home", has created clubs of listeners, "the family of Radio Maryja" where they cultivate traditional values, or rather the attitude of defence of traditional values, and get popularity by organizing prayers and support for the poor. While

[14] ibid., Article 38, p.14

the radio avoids directly antisemitic expressions, on many occasions they have not distanced themselves from listeners who called and talked about the Jewish plot to undermine Poland. Even more common are veiled references, as for example the expression "in Poland there is a fifth column coming from *the* national minority", which is code for the Jews. The radio and the recently created TV station, together with the daily newspaper run by the same circle, work with anti-European, traditionally Catholic politicians.[15]

The battles have one common denominator; the question to what extent should the religious community of the dominant Catholic Church be separate from the political realm? Should the teachings of the Church be binding for all? The key question was asked already several years ago – when things were not that clear – by the remarkable priest Józef Tischner; does the Church want political power in the state? It has been progressively clearer that the conservatives in the Catholic Church cannot imagine that the state laws may be not subordinated to Church values and principles.

This description of the anti-liberal offensive is quite frightening. It sounds familiar. Almost automatically the anti-liberal attitudes described above are assumed to be antisemitic. I also tend to make the assumption. I know, however, that this is not always true. Some church conservatives are clearly not antisemitic. For example, John Paul II was often on the conservative side warning against Western nihilism, but it would be a serious abuse to see his views as giving any support to antisemitism. What is more, I have not described *the* Polish church, but rather a part of the divided Polish church.

Yes, the defenders of the faith against all kinds of enemies form just a part of the Polish Church. Not only because of the new trends

[15] It must be added that in the more extreme circles of radical nationalists, anti-liberal and anti-European attitudes are explicitly antisemitic. To quote a radical nationalist weekly "*Nasza Polska*" of 1998, Poland is in danger because of "the bowing to (or rather, fawning upon) arrogant rule of madly anti-Polish Jewish chauvinists, and submissive acceptance of the dictatorship of Berlin and Brussels."

in the Church mentioned earlier but also because of concrete moves of Catholic leaders. Archbishop Gocłowski of Gdansk rebuked Father Jankowski of his city for unacceptable statements. True, Father Jankowski remained an influential figure, but he could not claim to represent the official position. Recently the archbishop removed him from the position of parish priest. It must be stressed that the move was prompted not by the views the priest expressed, but by the "moral disorder" in the parish where young men received money from the priest and engaged in suspicious activities.

Some bishops, like Bishop Pieronek, head of the Catholic Academy in Krakow, and Archbishop Życiński of Lublin, a well known philosopher, have strongly criticized "Radio Maryja", and a special commission of the Episcopate has been established to study the problem. No clear results have emerged, probably because some bishops support the station. The two bishops also thanked the Batory Foundation for its activities. The majority of the bishops seem, however, to look with suspicion at liberal tendencies. The present chairman of the Conference of the Episcopate, Bishop Józef Michalik, represents the majority. He is known for both an anti-communist past, and his statement shortly after 1989 that "Catholics should vote for a Catholic, Jews for a Jew, Muslims for a Muslim etc." Although it could be just a rhetorical device it is quite surprising in the Polish context. It naturally connects to the opinion that there are many Jews in Poland today and many Jewish politicians. According to a recent survey, as many as 37% Poles believe that now in Poland "there are very many politicians of Jewish origin", and this is highly correlated with antisemitism.

In Autumn 1997, a delegation of Polish bishops went to Brussels and came back with a remarkable pro-European statement. They have been criticized from many corners for being too soft on the pernicious liberalism of the European Union. To quote Father Tischner again; up to 1989 the Polish Church was based on "bearing witness *against*": against communism and against limitations on freedom for religion. Now the transition to a free society on its way to integration with the West is difficult. The conservatives need to have an enemy against whom they can position themselves.

The conservative tendencies, often close to Archbishop Lefebvre's right-wing traditionalist attitude, represent just a part the Polish church, and naturally they form an even smaller part of the entirety of Polish life. Polish democracy is based on open minded people who are many; they seem to outweigh the anti-Western forces, especially among younger generations. And even more important, there are plenty of events of high calibre which include local civic leaders, leaders of the Catholic Church, and other denominations. They are sometimes reported by the media, but because nothing dramatic happens during them the national media devote to them at most brief mentions, and foreign media do not notice them at all. They happen not only in Warsaw, Krakow, Wroclaw and Poznań, but occasionally also in smaller towns, as in Toruń where "Radio Maryja" has its headquarters. This is what I mean by the two faces of Poland.

6. Accomplishments

There are several tangible accomplishments in the field of Christian-Jewish dialogue. It is impossible to list them all, so some example will suffice. The International Council at the Auschwitz-Birkenau Museum, chaired by former Minister of Foreign Affairs Władysław Bartoszewski and Professor Israel Gutman, both survivors of the camp and experts on World War II, has been a forum for dialogue. One of the important lessons I have learned from being there is the fact that differences can cut across religious or ethnic distinctions. For example, it took years to debate whether a quotation from the Bible was appropriate for a monument commemorating the victims. Most of us wanted a quotation from Job.

It was Dr. Maurice Goldstein, of blessed memory, the president of the International Auschwitz Committee, an umbrella organization of survivors, who was our main adversary. The issues are covered in Chapter 1. The official documents of the Roman Catholic Church together with those of the Polish Catholic Church are mentioned in Chapter 7.

6.1. The Polish Episcopate's Commission for Dialogue with Judaism

Established in 1986, it was reconstructed in 1996 to become a Council inside the Commission for Inter-religious Dialogue. First it was chaired by Bishop Henryk Muszyński, who later became Archbishop of Gniezno and served for one term as the vice-president of the Bishops' Conference. For several years it has been led by Archbishop Stanisław Gądecki of Poznań, who is at present the vice-chairman of the Bishops' Conference. I think that the elevated position of both chairmen testifies to the importance of the commission.

At first the commission dealt mostly with the Carmelite convent crisis.[16] Later it moved to the field of implementation of Vatican Council reorientation in teaching about Jews into the Catholic teaching. For members of the commission consultations with Jews are seen as natural and obvious, which was literally unthinkable a few decades ago.

The pastoral letter of the Polish Episcopate of November 30, 1990, has remained the most notable written achievement of the commission. It expressed not only the historic new official teachings on Judaism stemming from the declaration *Nostra Aetate* but also addressed some problems connected to Polish history, specifically the consequences of the fact that while the Shoah was committed by Germans it happened principally on Polish soil. The letter succeeded in overcoming much of the defensiveness, so common in Poland,

[16] See Chapter 1.

denying any Polish involvement in that tragedy. A priest told me that some people during private confession mentioned the sin of antisemitism. Even if this is exceptional, it seems highly significant.

Another major achievement of the Commission, and by extension of the Polish Church, is highly original and most noteworthy. The Day of Judaism has been established as a national event in the Polish Catholic Church. It is to be observed every year on January 17. It is the day before the Week of Prayers for Christian Unity. While the first initiative of this kind took place in Italy, it is only in Poland that it is meant to cover the whole country. The first time, in January 1998, which happened to be Saturday, a special visit was paid by Bishop Gądecki and accompanying persons, together with dozens of Catholics, to the Warsaw synagogue. The visitors were present at a *havdalah* ceremony. The day was only marked in some churches with a special sermon or other event, but an important first step was taken. Since then it has become a tradition. It is genuinely observed in relatively few churches, although special materials are published annually. In some cities, remarkable prayers, discussions, and artistic events are prepared, sometimes with massive participation. Always one city is chosen as the central place. They were, from 1998 to 2005 in turn, Warsaw, Krakow, Lublin, Wrocław, Łódź, Białystok, Poznań, and Katowice. I participated actively (presenting reflections and commentaries to fragments from the Torah and the Psalms, offering remarks on Jewish views of Christianity) in most of them and can testify to the good atmosphere.

Sometimes Christians other than Catholics participate as well – in accordance with the postulates of Father Michał Czajkowski, ecumenical theologian, and for several years one of the most outspoken Polish Catholic voices explaining the new Church teachings about Jews and Judaism. Father Stanisław Musiał, a Jesuit from Cracow who died in 2000, was another important author. From 1986 to 1995, he was the secretary of the Episcopate's Commission. He was instrumental in arranging the transfer of the Carmelite convent near Auschwitz.[17] He opposed anti-Semitism so strongly that he had to face strong and sometimes vicious opposition within his own Church. He was ordered not to speak in public about the controversy concerning the crosses at Auschwitz. It was, needless to say, very painful to him. Yet he never compromised his clear stand. To me he was almost a saint, a representative of Christianity at its best.

The Day of Judaism involves more and more events every year. In 2005, in Katowice, there were concerts, a public service in the Jewish prayer room led by Rabbi Michael Schudrich, Chief Rabbi of Poland, meetings in churches with Jewish participation (one was devoted to commentaries on the Binding of Isaac, with Jewish, Catholic, Protestant and Russian Orthodox contributions), a discussion in the Theological Faculty of the Silesian University, and more. It was truly impressive though, unlike in most previous events, no Jewish lecturer from abroad was invited. Goodwill was obvious, as usual. Only once did I encounter in the Day of Judaism an approach that clearly did not fit the modern dialogue. Namely, during the 2003 Day, in Białystok, the Catholic lecturer spoke about Divine grace, and said God's mercy for Jews means that they can still convert. It was shocking that this kind of approach, a rejection of modern-style dialogue, was presented on the occasion of the Day of Judaism. And there was no place there to express that shock. I initiated a polemic with him in a major Catholic weekly.[18] It was summed up by Rev. Czajkowski who stressed that Jews are not to be seen as "not-yet-Christians". The exchange has strengthened my conviction that the modern Christian-Jewish dialogue is a matter of attitude or approach rather than exclusively a matter of scholarship. We all have to deal with many traditional opinions and of scriptural statements, together with old interpretations, that express

17 See Chapter 1.

18 *Tygodnik Powszechny* Feb, 2, 2003, and subsequent issues.

no respect for the other side. We can either perpetuate them or try to overcome them without losing the main message of the tradition. The assumption that this is possible constitutes a point of departure for the practitioners of this modern dialogue.

Fortunately, attitudes can change. I met my opponent, Rev. Professor Henryk Witczyk, in March 2005, incidentally at a conference in honour of Rev. Professor Czajkowski, and I encountered good will that led quickly to mutual understanding.

The above incident has been an exception as far as the Day of Judaism events go. In fact, due to the change in the atmosphere there are more and more priests and clerics who want to learn about Jewish religion and Jewish experiences from a Jew. I have participated in many meetings as have some of my Jewish colleagues, notably the well-known journalist Konstanty Gebert[19]. A major problem with the Day of Judaism is that there is just a handful of Jews educated enough and willing to participate in the events. The Commission says that one can explore the Jewish roots of Christianity even without Jewish participation.

Among other initiatives of the Polish Episcopate in which I was involved was the sponsorship in the 1990s, jointly with American Jewish Committee, of an exchange program for theologians, American rabbis and Polish priests, who visited the other country and lectured to students at Catholic universities and Jewish institutions.

6.2. The Polish Council of Christians and Jews

Established in 1991, the Polish Council of Christians and Jews, affiliated to the International Council of Christians and Jews, is an association of individuals active in the field of Christian-Jewish dialogue in their own circles. Some of the most devoted dialogue practitioners belong to the Council, priests and teachers, journalists, students, members of various Christian and Jewish

[19] He was another leader of the Jewish Flying University in 1979-1981 (see the Introduction).

organizations. First the council was co-chaired by myself and Father Waldemar Chrostowski, who left the Council in 1998 in result of a controversy with the majority of us. It arose from his polemic with Father Stanislaw Musiał, who published a remarkable criticism of the bishops who, according to Musiał reacted too weakly to the antisemitic utterances of Father Jankowski. Father Chrostowski defended the bishops in a way that could only be understood as indirect support for the antisemitic arguments of Father Jankowski. After this, his position was held by Rev. Andrzej Zuberbier and, after his untimely death, I have been privileged to work with Father Professor Michał Czajkowski. The controversy has shown how fragile the dialogue can be. The crisis has been very instructive to me. Some people were very angry at Father Chrostowski, and others asked why we did not want to be in dialogue with someone whose views we did not accept. It has become clear to me that the problem lies in the concept of the Council for dialogue, and distinct visions of the dialogue itself. There are three options; first, dialogue can be a diplomatic meeting of representatives. Then, of course, everyone is accepted, and Father Chrostowski must have an important place. Second, dialogue can be an uninhibited exchange, or a therapy group. This is indeed needed, and every sensible person should be welcome, and he or she must have the right to express all their views and attitudes as everyone else. Only there can be no public expression of such a process. It must remain confidential. No chairmen are needed. Finally, dialogue can be participation in a common endeavour, and building of mutual support. This was the tacit assumption when the Council was formed.

Two annual events have been organized by the Council since 1992; first, the March of Prayer on the Sunday closest to April 19, the traditional day of commemoration of the Shoah in Poland. We go along the Memorial Path in Warsaw, from one monument to the Jews to another, beginning at the Ghetto Heroes Monument and ending at the Umschlagsplatz Monument, the place from where 300,000 Jews wee taken by train to the gas chambers in Treblinka death camp. In several places Jewish and Christian prayers are offered by clergy of various denominations, and we read Psalms in Polish together. Nothing else is said. The other annual event is the annual gathering in one Warsaw church on the Sunday closest to the Jewish holiday Simchat Torah. We listen to some explanations about Judaism, read Biblical texts in Hebrew and Polish, listen to Jewish and Christian comments to the verses, and listen to individual reflections, describing their way to the Christian-Jewish dialogue. Finally we sing and read Psalms together, and at the end sing together the well-known Hebrew song for Simchat Torah: "*sisu wesimchu besimchat Torah utnu kavod la-Torah*". This event is our most original achievement because we have found a way to do a special service combining education, celebration and prayer (but no standard liturgy, either Jewish or Christian), and we do it in a church. Some two dozen Warsaw Jews have taken active part so far.

Every year the Council presents the Figure of Reconciliation Award to individuals who live abroad and have made outstanding contributions to the Jewish-Christian dialogue in Poland. It has been presented to: Stephan Schreiner (Germany), Rabbi Byron Sherwin (USA), Sir Sigmund Sternberg (UK), Father John Pawlikowski (USA), Rabbi A. James Rudin (USA), Sister Dominika Zaleska (Switzerland), Tova Ben Tzvi (Israel), Sister Marie Therese Huget (France), Rabbi Michael Schudrich (USA/Poland), Father Manfred Deselaers (Germany/Poland), Halina Birenbaum (Israel), Jan Nowak-Jeziorański (USA/Poland), Jerzy Kluger (Italy), Rev. Hanspeter Heinz (Germany), and Rabbi Michael Signer (USA). Each of the recipients deserves a separate chapter. The last two men have helped led several seminars in Poland, with Polish, American, and German students, Christian and Jewish. Christian-Jewish religious issues were coupled with historical issues and a visit to Auschwitz. It produced a really good program.

Members of the Council are active participants in the events of the Day of Judaism. We also help to organize other events. Two that took place in 2004 are especially noteworthy. In Kielce we organized a meeting in the city hall. It was about Christian-Jewish dialogue in general but was important because of the background; the city still does not know how to cope with the legacy of the notorious pogrom of 1946. Fortunately, the issue is addressed by committed activists, notably Bogdan Białek, the Council's member. Another event took place in Sandomierz, where an inter-religious conference, organized by Leszek Tyboń, was supposed to help resolve the standstill with the paintings in the local churches presenting the blood libel.[20] The aim was not achieved but the conference was interesting. In addition to historians, Christians, and Jews, there were also Muslim representatives.

6.3. Other initiatives

In Poland there more and more initiatives to commemorate the former Jewish presence in various towns; they vary from the fencing of cemeteries to the participation of high school students in local or nationwide competitions in which thousands participate. While it is not a mature dialogue it is a hopeful wave, which forms a background to future dialogue.

Sometimes the events commemorating the Jewish neighbours from before World War II are held under the auspices of the Church. This has been the case in the Lublin area where Archbishop Życiński himself has participated, together with local Jews, in several impressive events of that kind, in Lublin, in Łęczna, and in other localities.

Perhaps the most comprehensive event of that kind has been organized since 2002 in Otwock near Warsaw. A committee of

[20] See Chapter 7, sec. 5.

citizens, headed by Zbigniew Nosowski, the editor-in-chief of the Catholic monthly *Więź*, together with the local parish priest Father Wojciech Lemański, have held a series of educational events. Its focus is the march "from death to hope", which makes a series of stops in places important for former Jewish life as well as in the convent where a number of Jewish children were hidden during the war.

The monthly *Więź* was most interested in "Dabru Emet" declaration. It organized, together with the Polish Council of Christians and Jews, a seminar on the issues of the declaration, with the participation of one of its authors, Professor David Novak, and an important Jewish theologian Irving Greenberg. Another meeting on the declaration was organized in Krakow with the participation of another of its authors, Rabbi Michael Signer. In Krakow, there is another permanent centre of intellectual life where Polish Jewish themes are discussed in a penetrating manner. It is the "Judaica Foundation" on Meiselsa Street, directed by Dr. Joachim Russek, housed in a former synagogue building, a ruin that has been completely rebuilt. Many local cultural centres in Poland are located in former synagogues, which natural settings for classes on Jewish topics. These and other Polish cultural centres organize events, which include concerts, exhibitions, lectures, workshops (for example the workshop on Jewish papercuts or on Hebrew calligraphy, by my wife Monika Krajewska, has been offered not only in Warsaw but also in Włodawa, Morąg, Przysucha, and Karczew). This is educational, not dialogue proper. By far the most important cultural happening of this category, and the only one that can be called a genuine dialogue event, is the annual Festival of Jewish Culture in Krakow. The high quality concerts, exhibitions, lectures, workshops, excursions attract crowds, including tourists from many countries. The musical performances are of top quality, presented by genuine creators of contemporary Jewish music, mostly from America. Unlike most other Jewish festivals, in Poland and elsewhere, that easily fall into kitsch, for example by presenting actors acting as Jews, the Krakow Festival, under the charismatic leadership of Janusz Makuch, is always genuine: the performers show what they do in their real lives, teachers present themes they really care about. The unique atmosphere created then enables contacts and the background for dialogue as almost nothing else in contemporary Poland.

7. Towards the Future: a New Atmosphere and New Challenges.

Despite the growth of political right wing and conservative feelings in the Church, a new atmosphere in Catholic-Jewish relations is obvious. It makes me feel that I participate in a growing mainstream development in Poland. The progress is, to be sure, not without problems. For example, I know of a Catholic university where a few years ago there were many more lectures about Judaism than now.

Our dialogue is important for fundamental reasons, as it is in the rest of Europe and in America. It is also essential for us as a means to reduce antisemitism. In addition, it can be practically useful, also for Jews. After all, the church started restitution of former church property several years ago. (Incidentally, this has provoked criticism of what was perceived as the church's greed for property.) The Jewish community has also worked towards the restitution of former Jewish communal property, on the basis of legislation of May 1997. Co-operation of Jews and Christians in this area is not inconceivable.

Everywhere the inter-religious dialogue involves Muslims. This creates a new, difficult dimension. In Poland it has been hardly present, although there are some examples, as in the Sandomierz conference just mentioned. There have been contacts of the Catholic Church and of Polish Jews with those Muslims who belong to the centuries-old minority of Polish Tartars. They are assimilated and differ culturally from most Muslim immigrants. The latter are few in number in Poland, and nothing comparable to the communities in Western Europe which have caused problems. Also, little of the new anti-Semitism, connected with anti-Israeli positions, is present in Poland. And we can point to a remarkable pro-Zionist *fatwa* proclaimed in the 1930s by the Polish Mufti Jakub Szynkiewicz!

I believe that Christian-Jewish dialogue is an essential fragment of a variety of dialogues needed for a better future of our planet. The Christian "theology of Judaism" is being developed in the West, and it is in increasingly present in Poland. Books are being published and lecturers come; for instance Jacques Dupuis, SJ, promoted his book shortly before his death. For us Jews, Christian-Jewish dialogue presents a similar challenge. The Polish Pope referred to Jews as the Christians' "elder brothers" in faith. Now, if taken seriously, this term suggests that we should see Christians as our "younger brothers". A comprehensive vision that would be true to Jewish traditions and recognize a special brotherhood with Christians is yet to develop. This "Jewish theology of Christianity" is postulated by some thinkers in the USA, UK, and Israel. The most original attempts have been proposed by Rabbi Irving Greenberg.

Poland can have a role in the historic developments in the Christian-Jewish dialogue. After all, this is a most important place in Jewish history, and a very important country for the worldwide Catholic Church, as it was both the home of Pope John Paul II and the home of so many Jews over the centuries; and today is still the home of some Polish Polish Jews.

Index

Stanisław Krajewski, PhD, teaches at the Department of Philosophy of the University of Warsaw.

One of the leaders of Jewish renewal in Poland, he is a member of the board of the Union of Jewish Communities in Poland. He has been co-chairman of the Polish Council of Christians and Jews, and in the mid-1990s served on the board of the International Council of Christians and Jews. Member of the International Council of the Auschwitz-Birkenau Museum and Memorial from its creation, since 1992 he has been the American Jewish Committee's Poland consultant.

Krajewski is the author of articles in the field of logic, philosophy, Judaism, and Christian-Jewish dialogue. Among his recent publications are the books (in Polish): *Gödel's Theorem and Its Philosophical Interpretations: from Mechanism to Post-modernism* (Warsaw, 2003), and *54 Commentaries to the Torah for Even the Least Religious Among Us* (Austeria, Cracow, 2004).

Stanisław Krajewski

Title: Poland and the Jews:
Reflections of a Polish Polish Jew

Editing manager
Małgorzata Ornat

Text editing by
Jaime Ashworth

Photography on page 244 by
Monika Krajewska

Cover design by
Magdalena Koziak

Compose by
Irek Lipko

ISBN: 83-89129-22-1

Wydawnictwo Austeria
Klezmerhojs sp. z o.o.
Szeroka 6, PL 31-053 Kraków
phone +48 12 411 12 45
e-mail: austeria@austeria.pl
www.austeria.pl

Wydanie I
Kraków 2005